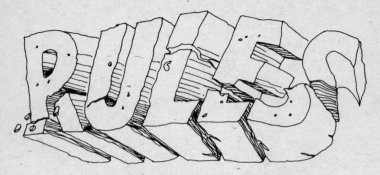

WHO NEEDS THEM?

by Ethel Barrett

A Regal Venture Book
A Division of G/L Publications
Glendale, California, U.S.A.

Second Printing, 1975
Third Printing, 1976

Published by Regal Books Division, G/L Publications
Glendale, California 91209
Printed in U.S.A.

Library of Congress Catalog Card No. 73-90623
ISBN 0-8307-0282-2

CONTENTS

This book may be used by teachers and students as a resource for the G/L Bible study *Adventures with New Leaders* (Course 53). Available from your church supplier.

RULES—
RULES!
WHO NEEDS
THEM?

Auugh.

But wait a minute.

Let's face it.

They're here to stay.

And if you're "alive 'n breathing" you're going to come to grips with them.

This is a story of people who came to grips with rules, each in his own way. There was the one who was born to be a leader—but he forgot he was supposed to *work* at it. And the one who had to stay on the sidelines—but she found out that God was there too. And the one who got off to a smashing start—but then he ran out of gas.

There were those who broke the rules and those who just "bent" them a little—and those who wanted to throw them out altogether and start over.

And there were those who kept them.

And where was all this going on?

In the Promised Land!

God had delivered the Israelites from Egypt. Moses had brought them *to* the Promised Land. Joshua had brought them *in*.

All this was going on after they'd been there awhile.

And what does this have to do with *you?*

Well, the Bible compares the Christian walk with contests and races and games.

"Play fair!"

"Give the other fellow a break!"

"Train, train, train!"

"Practice, practice, practice!"

"Go, go, go!"

"The name of the game is hard work!"

"KEEP THE RULES!"

Ah, yes. Keep the rules.

For the way we handle the rules of the game is often the way we handle the rules of life.

Read on.

See if you can recognize yourself.

When you see a word with a small number
after it (like: problem[1])
   look
     at
       the
         bottom
           of
             the
               page

1. Something you have to figure out.

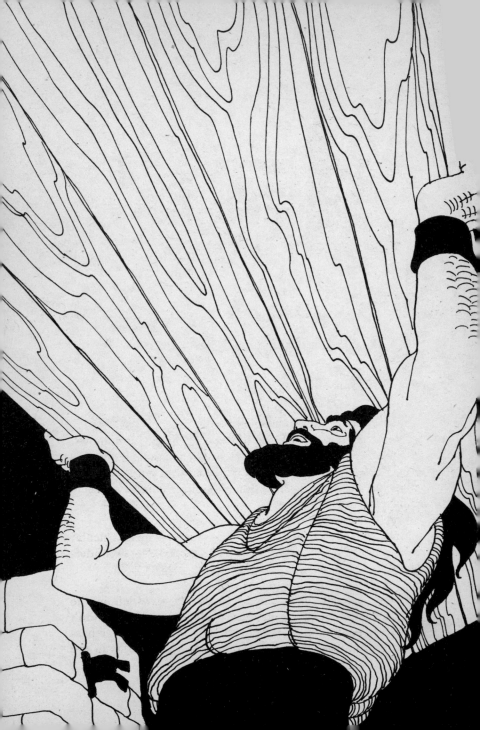

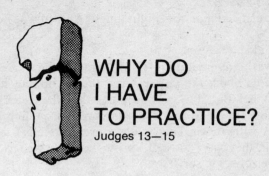

WHY DO
I HAVE
TO PRACTICE?
Judges 13—15

"Some People Just Have It Made"

"Some people just seem to be naturally great. You know—Mr. Wonderful. Big muscles, great talent, and all the rest of it. They never seem to have to work at anything. All the prizes just drop in their laps. Sometimes they don't even seem to have to obey the rules."

Well, so it seems, sometimes—so it seems.

And if you'd seen the man in this story on this particular night, you would have thought he was indeed "Mr. Wonderful."

It was midnight. The city of Gaza lay sprawled in the darkness, silent and snug inside its walls. And safe? Couldn't be safer! The double gates were securely locked by huge bars that ran from post to post on either side. The guards in the watch towers blinked sleepily out into the darkness, and then nodded and zzzzzzzzzz . . .

Quiet, quiet, all but the night bugs. And of course the zzzzzzzzzz. . . .

When suddenly—

There was a resounding THUMP against the gates, and they quivered under the impact. And then a ripping sound. It couldn't be! But it was. The posts that the gates were attached to were being torn from the ground, pulling earth and stones with them. Then with a great GRUNT and a giant HUP, they were hoisted up on—horses? A chariot? A huge carrier of some sort?

No—on the shoulders of a man!

And before the goggling guards could come out of their stupor, this man marched off, dragging the gates with him, posts and all—and disappeared into the darkness!

Surely a man like that never had to practice. Or train. Or build himself up. Or indeed even keep any rules. He already had it made.

They Have It Made Before They're Even Born

It seemed to be that way, with this man.

Long, long before that night when the gate was yanked right out of its socks, and before that man was even born, something happened that was absolutely astonishing. It happened to an Israelite woman who was working in a field. She worked with one eye on the crops, and the other eye looking for the enemy. For these were troubled times in Israel. For forty years, the Philistines had been swooping down upon them, stealing their crops and in general making their lives miserable. This day was like any other. Until suddenly—

Something happened that sent her scurrying off to her husband.

"Manoah!" she cried. "I've been talking to a stranger. I don't know where he came from. He was just suddenly *there.*"

Manoah straightened up and looked at her in fear.

"He was not a Philistine," she said. "He was not like anybody I've ever seen before."

"Well?"

"Well, he told me that we were going to have a child. A son."

Manoah stared at her in disbelief. They had been married many years and had given up all hope of having any children.

"A son," she said again. "But that's not all. He will begin to deliver us from the Philistines."

This was incredible. This was astonishing. This was wonderful!

"Where'd he go?" Manoah wanted to know.

"I don't know," she said. "He was just *gone*—as suddenly as he came. I don't know where he came from, or his name, or anything about him. He was not like any other man. His face was radiant. And oh, he gave me a set of rules to live by. Both for myself—and for the child when he is born." And she told her husband what the rules were.

He stared at her for a moment. Had the sun's heat affected her mind? Or had this really happened?

"Then we shall pray," he said finally, "that the stranger will come visit us again. I must ask him how we are to bring up such a child—a child who will grow up to deliver us from the Philistines."

His wife had already told him what the rules were, but being a man, he had to find out for himself. And being a good wife, she kept quiet.

Well, Manoah prayed. And his prayer was answered. For, a few days later, his wife came running to him in the fields again. "He's back!" she cried. "The stranger is back! Come see him!"

Manoah ran back with his wife. And sure enough, the stranger was there. "Tell us," Manoah said, "how shall we bring up this child? Can you give us any special instructions?"

The stranger looked at Manoah intently. "It is exactly as

I told your wife," he said. And he repeated the same set of rules.

There was something about this stranger that set Manoah atrembling.

"Please stay," he cried, "so we can get you something to eat. And what is your name?"

"I'll stay," the stranger said, "but not to eat. If you want to bring food, make a sacrifice to the Lord. And don't even ask my name. For it is secret."

Manoah took a young goat and some cereal, and laid them on a rock to make the sacrifice. And suddenly, everything seemed to happen at once.

A flame came shooting out of the rock and burnt the sacrifice. And the mysterious stranger went right up into the flame—and disappeared!

Manoah and his wife fell on their faces. It was only then that they realized that they had actually been talking to an angel of the Lord.

"We'll die," Manoah moaned, "for we have seen God!"

"Nonsense," said his wife. "If God were going to kill us, He wouldn't have promised us a son."

Of course that made sense.

And of course it all came to pass. They had a son. And they named him Samson.

And it did indeed look as if he "had it made" before he was even born. He was born to be a great leader, and to deliver the Israelites from their enemies, the Philistines. BUT—

There was a set of rules attached to the deal. And this is what they were:

His mother was to drink no wine or strong drink, or eat anything unclean. Why? Because Samson was to be a *Nazirite*. And Nazirites were people who dedicated themselves to God. They promised God they would not drink wine or strong drink or eat anything unclean. And the sign that they were keeping this promise was—

They never, never cut their hair.

4

Some people became Nazirites for a few weeks, or months. Samson was to be a Nazirite for *all of his life.*

Samson was born to be a great leader. But he was supposed to *work at it.*

"I've Got All This Talent— I Must Be Somebody Special!"

Yes indeed.

The point is not to get cocky about it.

Thankful, yes. Cocky, no.

Samson knew from the beginning—even as a boy—that he had a great talent. The Bible tells us, "The child grew, and the Lord blessed him."[1] He had a clever mind. And a very strong body. Tales of his great strength spread until, in time, all the Israelites knew about it. And the Philistines knew about it too. And so it wasn't too long before Samson began to figure that he was indeed "somebody special."

But Aren't Those the Guys Who Always Get Noticed?

Yes, indeed. Samson got noticed all right. He was a glittering, dashing, flashing, swaggering, swashbuckling hero. And his feats of "daring-do" would have made headlines both in the Israelite Daily News and the Philistine Tattler.

It started with the lion . . .

Samson was on his way to the Philistine city of Timnah with his father and mother, to make arrangements for his wedding. And he was either running ahead of his parents or lagging behind, when it happened.

The lion was prowling through a vineyard outside Timnah when he heard Samson coming. He crept stealthily to the edge of the path and waited for Samson to come closer. And then he roared, his eyes spitting fire. And then he crouched and got ready to spring.

And that was the last thing the lion remembered.

1. Judges 18:24.

For he never got a chance to spring at Samson. Samson sprang at *him*. And tore him from stem to stern. *With his bare hands.*

Samson rejoined his parents. But he did not tell them what happened.

And then there was the riddle . . .

It all came about when Samson went to Timnah again with his parents. But the wedding had already been arranged and this time they were on their way to the wedding feast. Samson left his parents long enough to go off the path a bit. And there, sure enough, was the carcass of the dead lion, lying right where he had killed it. The sun had dried it up, and of all things, a swarm of bees had built a hive inside it—and the hive was filled with honey. Samson scraped some of the honey out in his hand and ate it as he went, and gave some to his mother and father. But he did not tell them where he had got it, and for a good reason. As a Nazirite, he was not supposed to touch a dead body. This was one of the rules.

And that was how the business of the riddle started. Samson thought of the riddle while he was at his wedding feast. And he sprang it on thirty young men who were his guests. "I have a riddle for you," he said. "If you can guess it, I'll give you thirty plain robes and thirty fancy robes. But if you can't guess it, then you must give the robes to me."

Sounded like a splendid idea. "Right on!" they said. So out of his adventures with the lion and the honey, Samson made up his riddle. And this is what it was: "Food came out of the eater and sweetness out from the strong."

Well, three days later, they were still trying to figure it out.

By the fourth day, they were desperate. "Get the answer from Samson," they said to his new bride. "Or we'll burn down your father's house. With you in it! We weren't invited to this party to be made poor, you know!"

6

Well, that wasn't a very delicate thing to say to a new bride, but then the Philistines were not very delicate people.

It's no way to start a marriage—to break down in tears. But Samson's new bride was desperate. "You don't love me at all!" she wailed. "You hate me! You've told a riddle to my people and you haven't told me the answer!"

"I haven't told even my own mother and father the answer!" he said. "Why on earth should I tell you?"

Why indeed?

Well, she didn't dare tell him why indeed.

So she just kept on wailing. Which is saying a great deal, for the wedding feast lasted seven days. And she never stopped wailing and coaxing during most of that time. Then, on the seventh day—

"Enough!" he cried. "Stop it!" And he told her the answer.

At last the week of the wedding feast was over. It was the evening of the seventh day. "Well?" said Samson to the thirty young men. "The answer to my riddle?" And to his astonishment they not only had an answer—they had the *right* one! "What is sweeter than honey?" they said, "and what is stronger than a lion?" Samson looked at them, his mouth hanging open. And then he looked at his bride. There was only one way they could have found out. She had told them!

Well, you never saw a wedding feast break up into such a muddle. Samson went down to the nearby town of Ashkelon, killed thirty Philistines, took their clothing, and gave it to the young men who had told the answer to his riddle. Then, in a rage, he left his bride and went home to live with his parents. And that was the end of the marriage feast. His bride got married all right, but not to Samson. She married the chap who had been his best man!

And *that's* how the foxes and the big fire came about.

What? You don't know about the foxes and the fire?

Well, it seems that along about harvest time, Samson cooled off. He took a young goat and a present to his bride and

7

ambled back to Timnah. But his bride's father wouldn't let him in the house. "I thought you hated her, Samson," the father said, "so I married her to your best man."

"Woooooaugggghhh!" said Samson. "You can't blame me for what happens now!"

That was when Samson waged his one-man war, using an army of three hundred. What? One-man war? Using an army of three hundred? Yes. Samson was the one man. And the army of three hundred he used were—foxes!

Yes. He actually rounded up three hundred foxes and corralled them alongside the grain fields of the Philistines. Then quietly, quietly, he wrapped cloth around sticks and dipped them in oil to make them into torches. Then carefully, carefully, he tied the foxes' tails together, two by two. And then—Pfffff!—he lighted the torches. Pffffft!—pffffft!—PFFFFFT! And then—turned the foxes loose, to run wildly into the grain fields.

Fire!

And the Philistines awakened and ran in a great scramble to their fields.

FIRE!!!

And the grain was burning, and the olive trees! And the sky was lighted up with it! Phew!

It had come about in a most peculiar and roundabout way, but Samson, single-handed, had put Israel's enemies to flight.

But Is This Any Way to Get Noticed?

Yes indeed, Swashbuckling Samson got noticed all right. In fact the Philistines were noticing him with such gusto that he had to run for his life!

It's true that he had made the first breakthrough in forty years into the enemy ranks. But he had also fudged a little on his Nazirite vows. He had never cut his hair, so he *looked* like a Nazirite. But there were times when he didn't *act* like one.

Hail the Conquering Hero?!!??

Breakthrough! At long last, after forty years, someone had dared to defy the Philistines! Israel's strong man—Samson!

Israel, at long last, had a champion. Would Samson get a welcoming parade? Would they carry him on their shoulders and come out in great throngs to welcome him?

They would not.

And apparently he didn't expect them to, for he went back to Judah and hid in the hills. Now the men of Judah were his own people. True, they were of a different tribe.[2] But still, they were Israelites. Wouldn't they help him?

They would not.

For the awful truth is, they had sunk so low and turned so far away from God, that they weren't looking for a champion. For if they expected God to help them they would have to repent. And they weren't willing to repent. They had all suffered from the cruelty of the Philistines. But they were so bogged down in their idol-worship that it was easier to put up with the Philistines than it was to rally around the champion and fight them.

Sin had certainly taken the ginger out of them.

So three thousand of them—all spineless jellyfish—tracked Samson down. God had sent them a deliverer and they didn't know him when they saw him. "Whatever do you think you're doing!" they bellowed. "Don't you know that the Philistines are our rulers? Why don't you let well enough alone? Now they're after you. Thousands of them. They're camped all over the place. We've come to bind you and turn you over to them. It's the only sensible thing to do."

He stared at them a moment. "Promise me that you won't attack me yourselves," he said, "and I'll let you bind me." Did he say this because he was afraid of them? No. He said it because he knew that if they attacked him, he could wipe

2. Samson was of the tribe of Dan. Remember?

9

them all out with one blow. Samson was rough on the Philistines, but he did not want to attack his own people.

WHAT Victim?

Samson was done for? Well, it certainly looked like it. They bound him all right. With brand new cords that had never been used before. And they hauled him off to the Philistines.

The roar that went up from the Philistines when they saw him coming was terrible to hear. It rose like thunder to the skies. And from the sound of it, it was quite clear that when they got hold of Samson they would tear him limb from limb. Why here was Israel's great strong-man, all tied up like a package, waiting to be delivered right into their hands. Why they'd tear him—

Hup!!! What was this?

Rippppp! And what was *this?*

The Lord gave Samson a sudden mighty burst of strength. And with one mighty twist, Samson broke the new ropes as if they had been #60 thread out of a sewing box!

For a moment, the Philistines were too horrified to move. And then Samson picked up the jawbone of a dead donkey and began to swing.

They moved.

It was one mad scramble, and in every direction. God had made Samson so strong that he was pretty hard to *out*-scramble. And before he was through swinging, a thousand of them were killed. He piled them up in heaps.

It was another single-handed victory. But did the Israelites cheer? The Bible does not tell us they did. Samson had to sing his own victory song:

"Heaps upon heaps,
All with a donkey's jaw!
I've killed a thousand men,
All with a donkey's jaw!"

And the Israelites went skulking off. They were no closer to God than they'd been before.

10

From that time on, though, Samson was a power in Israel. The Bible tells us that he was Israel's judge for the next twenty years. It was toward the end of that time that he ripped up those gates at Gaza.[3]

BUT.

The Philistines still controlled the land.

"I Want to Be Great—But Do I Have to Work at It?"

Samson was great—no doubt about it. And he was a Nazirite—no doubt about it. But there was one little problem.

He didn't work at it.

He kept fudging. And breaking the rules. He neglected his training. He was so strong and so great that he never felt the need to practice. And he never felt the need to deny himself.

Samson, alas, had a habit of taking what he wanted whether it was good for him or not. He never did cut his hair. So it was true, he did *look* like a Nazirite. But all too often, he didn't *act* like one.

"Yeah—But Some People Do Get By, Don't They?"

"Some people fudge a little, and break some of the rules. Some people break a lot of the rules. And they seem to get by. Some of them are leaders, too. Yeah—even the leaders do that, and they seem to get by."

Oh, sure. They get by for a while. Sometimes it may seem that they get by for a long, long while. If you'd seen Samson rip up those gates at Gaza and walk off with them on his shoulders, you would have thought he was Mr. Wonderful indeed. Surely a man like that never had to practice. Or build himself up. Or keep any rules. He already had it made.

Well, didn't he?

3. His enemies knew he was in the city. They were waiting to catch him when he came out in the morning. But he fooled them and came out that night—gates and all!

Well, *Do* They?

Don't be too sure. The game wasn't over yet. There was more to come. We'll find out about it in the next chapter.

And you can't go on breaking rules forever . . .

What About You?

Make a list of the abilities that God has given you.

What? You can't think of a list? You can't even think of *one?* Oh, come on now. This is no time to be modest. Nobody will see the list but you and the Lord. He has given everybody the ability to do *something*. Even you.

You've thought of something?

Good.

Now make a list of the things you are doing about it. What? You aren't doing anything about it? Well then, make a list of the things you *should* be doing about it. For God doesn't give you an ability on a silver platter, fully developed. He expects you to work at it. And while you're working at it, don't forget who gave it to you in the first place.

Now suppose—just *suppose*—you think you have such great ability that you don't *have* to work at it. You're just so terrific there's no need to practice. You're already the best there is. Wouldn't it be a pretty good idea if you ran that through again and looked at it more carefully?

Back in the days of Nehemiah, the Jews built up the walls of Jerusalem. They all had abilities and talents galore to do the job. But it never would have been done, except that "the people had a mind to work" (Neh. 4:6, *KJV*). And the apostle Paul tells us: "No athlete is ever awarded the wreath of victory unless he has kept the rules" (2 Tim. 2:5, *TCNT*).

So you see, this isn't something your mother says. Or your father. Or your teacher. God says it.

With this in mind, it might be a good idea for you to go over your list again. Maybe it'll look different to you this time.

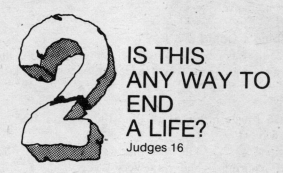

IS THIS ANY WAY TO END A LIFE?

Judges 16

So You Think You Have It Made?

There was no doubt about it. Samson seemed to be living a charmed life. He was a walking example of "How to Succeed Without Trying." He had superhuman strength at his command when he needed it. And if he could be a Nazirite by just having the outside appearance of one—in his case his long hair—why bother working at it? All he had to do was show everybody the outward signs. After all, that was all that mattered.

Well, wasn't it?

Of course. Just keep up the outside appearances and you have it made. After all, this had been working for Samson so far. And it looked as if it would be working for the rest of his life. He had everything going for him. He was well established as a judge in Israel. True, the Philistines would

15

have given anything to capture him. Preferably alive. But for years they'd been hoping to do this. And the answer was—not a chance!

"Everything's Going My Way"

This could have been Samson's theme song. For indeed everything *was* going his way. He was in love with a Philistine woman.

Again?!?

Yes. He'd been in love with Philistine women before and gotten away with it.

Her name was Delilah. And she was fun to be with, and very, very charming—and very, very lovely . . .

Nothing Can Trip You Up Now!—???

In the valley of Sorek, west of Jerusalem, the woman sat on a stone bench in the courtyard of her house. She had five guests—five very important guests. They were VIP's—five Philistine lords, in fact. The woman was dressed to the teeth, for they were there on very important business.

You guessed it. Her name was Delilah.

What? *Samson's* Delilah?

The very same.

And she was not only very, very charming and very, very lovely—she was also very, very *greedy*—and very, very *underhanded.*

And she was, at the moment, in the process of making a deal.

The five VIP's were speaking.

"We are prepared to pay you eleven hundred pieces of silver[1] for this information."

"—Each of us, that is."

"That will total fifty-five hundred pieces of silver."[2]

1. About four thousand dollars.
2. Twenty thousand dollars.

"Which is quite a tidy sum, *quite* a tidy sum."

Yes, indeed it was.

Delilah smiled prettily and declared that she would do her best to get the information they wanted. They agreed to provide some men to help her. And she made arrangements for those men to hide in an inner chamber the very next time Samson came to visit.

And what was the information they wanted? Why, they wanted Delilah to find the secret of Samson's great strength! And what's more, Delilah promised to do it! So you can see right off that D-E-L-I-L-A-H spells "trouble," and that Samson is in for it.

Or Can It?

The drama begins the very next time Samson came to visit. Delilah was clever enough to talk by "circumlocution"[3] for a while. Then she got to the point.

"Tell me, Samson," she finally said, *"please* tell me—what is the secret of your great strength? And what would you have to be bound with to subdue you? Is there *anything* you could be bound with so you couldn't break loose?"

Now Samson was not stupid. Rambunctious,[4] yes. But not stupid. He must have known that she was up to some sort of mischief. After all, he was an expert on mischief himself, and it takes one to know one. But he had nothing to fear. He had spent his life outwitting the Philistines. So why not play her little game? And tease her a bit. What harm would it do? Certainly no one could trip *him* up. No one had been able to yet. He could amuse himself at her expense!

"If you were to bind me with seven raw-leather bowstrings," he said, his tongue in his cheek and his fingers crossed behind his back, "I would become as weak as any ordinary man."

---

3. That's talking around in circles. Good word! Try it on your mother. You pronounce it like "sir-come-low-Q-shun." Get it?
4. Knocker-downer-dragger-outer.

17

And before he hardly had the words out of his mouth, those rascals in the inner chamber were sending out for some.

And later while Samson was sleeping, sure enough, Delilah bound him with the bowstrings, tugging on the knots with all her strength. At last it was done. And then—

"Samson!" she cried, wringing her hands. "The Philistines are upon you!"

Oh, HO. So she was going to play her little game to the end. Well, he'd play it along with her. He stood up. And with one little tug, the bowstrings seemed to melt as if they'd been burned by fire.

Now the rascals in the inner chamber were not stupid either. They were not about to pounce on Samson until they were sure those knots were going to hold. And so when they realized that he had snapped his bonds, they stayed hidden where they were. They had no desire to tangle with him. And so the evening passed and Samson went home. It had been pleasant, and Delilah had had her little joke, he thought. And he had had the last laugh.

But Delilah had not been joking. And the little drama was not over.

The Long Slide Down

Sure enough, she tried again.

"Samson, you're making fun of me. You told me a lie! *Please* tell me the secret of your strength—and how you may be captured!"

"Well, then," he said, "if I'm tied with new ropes that have never been used—I will be as weak as any ordinary man."

Delilah went at it, her eyes boggling in her head at the thought of that twenty thousand dollars. This time he was tied with brand new ropes.

The rascals in the inner chamber were waiting—waiting—

"Samson!" Delilah cried, "The Philistines are upon you!"

But Samson s-n-a-p-p-e-d the ropes as if they were sewing

18

thread! And the five rascals in the inner room stayed there and gnashed their teeth.

But Delilah had not given up.

Sliding—

"Samson," she sighed, "You've mocked me again. You've told me more lies. I *beg* you to tell me the truth—how can you *really* be captured."

Ah, HA. She was giving it still another try.

By now it was clear that it was more than a game. And this time Samson came about as close to being a smart aleck as it was possible to get. It was like driving along a road on the edge of a cliff and seeing how *close* you could get to the edge—when the smart thing to do would be to stay as far *away* from the edge as possible.

This time he took *the very sign and symbol* of his Nazirite vow and risked it as if it were a worthless thing. "If," he said (and you'll find this hard to believe), "if you'll take my hair and weave it right into that piece of cloth on your loom—then I will surely lose my strength."

Now that was about as cocky as you could get.

It doesn't seem possible that he would say a thing like that. But he did. And what's more, she took him up on it.

A little later, and while he was dozing, she set up her loom for weaving. And very deliberately wove Samson's hairs right into the cloth, as if they were threads! And he stood a chance of being a part of somebody's suit—plain or fancy! His hair was a pretty substantial part of whatever she was weaving!

But before this happened, he leapt to his feet, pulling the loom and the posts that held it, right out of the floor!

The rascals in the inner chamber stayed hidden. They were seething.[5]

And Samson? He stalked off with the loom and cloth—*and his hair* still attached to him. And even though he had to

5. They were blowing their tops, all bent out of shape.

do some ripping out of some cloth to get his hair back, he was still unabashed.[6]

He still thought he was superman.

And Sliding—

Delilah, however, was beginning to get desperate. That twenty thousand dollars! Oh, woe! *"Samson!"* she wailed, and *"Samson!"* she whined, "You've mocked me and told me lies and made fun of me three times now! When *will* you tell me?" This went on for days. And it was beginning to wear him down.

And finally he was worn out with her tears and her pleading.

You see, once you get in the habit of just "sliding by" you get pretty good at it. He'd been sliding by and going his own way for many years now. The only thing he'd ever really worked on was making mistakes. And now he was about to make the biggest one of his life.

He was overdue for it.

And Slidin-n-n-n-g—!

In one gigantic burst of carelessness and foolishness and disregard of God—he broke down and told her the real secret of his strength. "I'm a Nazirite," he said. "I was dedicated to God before I was born. And as a sign of this dedication, my hair could never be cut. If my hair is ever cut—if that sign of my dedication to God is gone—then I will lose my strength."

Deliiah stopped whining. Her heart began to beat like a trip hammer. She knew—she *knew*—that he was at last telling the truth. The twenty thousand dollars was as good as hers.

She told the five rulers of the Philistines as much. And they began to set the stage for trapping Samson. The end of the drama was drawing near. The rest would be easy.

6. He hadn't "lost his cool."

20

It was.

The Philistines had already sent for a barber to cut his hair.

AND SLIDING—

He already had it made. Didn't he? Samson snoozed on comfortably. He'd *always* had it made. All that strength, all that ability—he would always have it made whether he fudged or not. And he would always be great whether he worked at it or not.

"Samson! Samson!" It was Delilah shouting at him.

"Samson! Wake up! The Philistines are upon you!"

He struggled to his feet. "Whatever she's done," he thought, "I'll shake myself free as I've always done before."

Samson didn't know that the game was over. For it is one of the saddest verses of the Bible that "Samson did not know that the Lord had departed from him."[7]

"Hup!" he blustered, as he had done so many times before. The Philistines had come out of hiding and they were swaggering into the room. "Hup!" he cried again, and crouched, ready to spar with them. And spar he did, with all his might. But as they overcame him, he realized with a great horror—that his strength was gone.

His strength was gone!

They held him down.

And bored out his eyes.

And dragged him off, into the darkness.

The "unfallable" Samson had fallen. The game was over.

—To the Very Bottom!

The city of Gaza sprawled in the moonlight as it had before. The gates were back on again, sound and secure. And the superman who had once torn them off was again inside the

7. Judges 16:20.

21

city. But this time he was in prison. And this time he was
blind, chained to the mill in the prison house.

The grain mill was made of two enormous stones shaped
like huge doughnuts. One rotated upon the other, and the
grain was crushed between the two. Ordinarily they were
pulled by blinded oxen or donkeys; this one was pulled by
blinded Samson.

Around and around he stumbled, dragging his chains behind him. Whether it was day or night no longer mattered—for
him it was dark, endlessly dark, all the time.

He thought of his life, and of the great talent and ability
God had given him, and how he had not worked at it, and
had finally thrown it all away. What a smart aleck he had
been! And now his strength was gone, and his power was
gone. And his position as Israel's leader had gone too. But
the worst thing of all was—God had left him. How many
times he had thought of his Israelite Nazirite vow, and how
he had thrown it away. And how he had despised it, and
finally broken it. And how many times he wished that it were
not so—that he could wake up and find it all a bad dream.

But it wasn't a bad dream. It was all true.

And he dragged wearily and endlessly around the grain
mill.

And his hair began to grow.

So You Thought You Had It Made

"Dagon!"

"Hail to our god Dagon!"

"Hail to our god of grain!"

"Our god Dagon has given Samson our enemy into our
hands!"

The city had been abuzz with excitement and preparation
for six days. And at last the great day was here. A gigantic
festival to celebrate the capture of Samson and to honor the
god Dagon!

The crowds were enormous. The tables were groaning like

sway-back horses under the load of goodies upon them. The choice seats, of course for the VIP's, were in the temple itself. The LIP's[8] were stashed away in balconies and out in the courtyard. The NIP's[9] had the bleacher seats, up on the roof. There were three thousand of them up there alone. Of course the five Philistine rulers who had started this whole mess were at the head table inside the temple. And the clink of glasses and the clank of silverware and the rattle of dishes and the bursts of laughter rose to the sky. Everyone was in excellent spirits. And then someone had a jolly idea.

"Bring Samson!" someone shouted, "that we might see him!"

"Go fetch Samson!"

"Bring him in that we might make sport of him and laugh at him!"

"Now! And make the evening complete!"

The thing caught on. Now everyone was shouting.

"Samson! We want Samson!"

One of the VIP's had already sent for Samson, and a young lad was leading him, even now, from the prison to the temple.

Finally, "He's coming!" someone said, and the word was passed on.

"He's coming!"

"He's coming! Here he comes!" It became a great shout.

"He's coming!!!"

You could hardly hear for the din, as he was led into the great hall. People in the balconies and people in the bleachers strained their necks to see.

—But This Isn't the Way You'd Planned It

Before him was a huge audience. Samson had always loved an audience. He had always loved to "show off." He had

8. Less important people.
9. Not important people.

always loved excitement. And here was all the excitement he could ever hope for in all his life.

He could hear it.

But it left him weak with sorrow. For his eyes were gone. And he wept, for he had refused God's love and he had taken God's talents and thrown them away. And now it was too late.

The din of the shouting was like thunder in his ears. He leaned over to the lad. "Where are the pillars?" he said. "Place my hands upon the pillars."

The lad put Samson's hands on the two large pillars that supported the roof.

"Now leave me alone," said Samson, "I want to rest a minute."

You Began to Care—Too Late

He just stood there, his hands on the pillars, crying with grief. And he remembered his Nazirite vow, made so many years ago—how he had been dedicated to God by his mother and father. He remembered all the times that God had helped him. He pressed his hands against the pillars, hard, and stood up straight. He raised his head. And cried out to God. "Lord God," he cried, "remember me, I pray You, and strengthen me, I pray You, only this once, oh, God, just this once!" And he took fast hold of the two pillars, and he pushed against them, one with his right hand and the other with his left—with all his might. He bent his body and strained against them— *with—all—his—might*—pushing the pillars, pushing—pushing—

Oh, NO!

There was a great ripping and a crashing as the pillars were forced apart. Huge timbers groaned and swayed and then came crashing down. And the drunken laughter turned to screams of horror. People scrambled over each other, pushing, shouting, trampling each other underfoot—

"The roof! The roof!"

The roof was giving away! The whole building seemed to sway crazily, and then—

There was a ripping and a crashing and a grinding—and the center of the roof caved in—and then *all* of it crashed down, huge timbers snapping like toothpicks! And people slid and clawed and lost their hold—and fell into the great hall below. And all these sounds melted into one great sound like thunder as if the earth itself were ripping apart. And the choking, blinding dust from the plaster and the bricks was everywhere.

The great temple of Dagon was a heap of rubble.

"Let me die with the Philistines!" Samson had cried.

He got his wish.

And those he had killed at the moment of his death were more than those he had killed in his whole lifetime.

Is This Any Way to End a Life?

It was one of the worst disasters the Philistines had known for many years. The news spread throughout the country. Streets were blocked off, and people streamed in from everywhere to see the mass of rubble that had once been the temple. And many of them searched for their dead friends and relatives. In the terrible confusion of cleaning up, no one noticed a few Israelites poking through the rubble. They were Samson's brothers and other relatives. They found him and got him out somehow.

No one tried to stop them.

And so Samson went home at last, to his father's house.

He'd had it made before he was born. He'd been born to be a great leader, but he hadn't bothered to work at it. He was a glittering, dashing, swaggering, swashbuckling hero. But he forgot that he had been dedicated and set apart for God. And he forgot where his great strength came from. And without God he was nothing.

Is this any way to live a life?

No. And Samson would have been the first to admit it.

25

What About You?

How do you want to end your life?

"How do I want to *end* my life? Don't rush me. I've hardly even *begun* it."

So it would seem. However, there's no guarantee how long your life's going to be. But there's no sense quibbling about it. Why don't you set down some goals for yourself? With the abilities God has given you, what do you think He wants you to be? And why don't you at least start working in that direction? It's a cinch that whether your life is long or short, God has a plan for it. And if you think you'll always be great whether you work at it or not—you may blow it.

So write down a few goals.

Now write down what you must do to achieve them.

Now get going. You're already years too late!

The apostle Paul says, ". . . I only want to *finish* the race, and *complete* the task which the Lord Jesus assigned to me . . ." (See Acts 20:24.)

DO I ALWAYS HAVE TO BE ON THE SIDELINE?

1 Samuel 1:1—2:10

The woman stumbled into the courtyard of the Tabernacle. She was crying so hard she could barely see where she was going. Before the entrance, she fell to her knees. And as she wept, she was also speaking without making a sound.

Eli the priest who was sitting at the door of the Tabernacle, watched her. She was behaving very strangely, very strangely indeed. Just weeping and muttering. Muttering to herself? Or was she talking to someone? What kind of nonsense was this? She must be drunk. Must she come here to drink? He stared at her, frowning, angry. "Must you come here to drink?" he demanded. "Throw away your wineskin. Be done with your drunkenness." Now that was no way to speak to a lady, no matter what she was doing. He could have been a little more tactful.

She looked up at him, her eyes streaming. "Oh, no, sir,"

29

she said, "I'm not drunk. And I'm not talking to myself. I'm pouring out my heart to the Lord. Please don't think that I'm some drunken—some drunk—" She couldn't finish.

"Praying, are you?" the priest said. "Well, in that case, cheer up! And may the Lord of Israel grant your request, whatever it happens to be."

Well, now, that was a little better.

"May your servant find favor in your sight," she said, which was a polite way of saying thank you. She got to her feet again, brushed off her robes, and turned and left.

Who was this woman? Whatever was she asking for? And why? And what was she doing there alone in the first place?

Do I Always Have to Be on the Sidelines?

Well, no one wants to be on the sidelines. We like to be right out there in first place, sailing through life in shining splendor, with everyone applauding.

If there was ever a woman who was on the sidelines, this woman was. And she didn't like it much either. That's why she was crying. Her name was Hannah. And she lived in the rocky hills of Ephraim about twelve miles away from the Tabernacle in the city of Shiloh. Elkanah was her husband. And what was her problem? The problem was that she was not his only wife. Elkanah had another wife. Her name was Peninnah. Well, it was fairly common for a man to have more than one wife back in those days. So what was the problem?

Well, the problem was, first, that Peninnah had some rosy, bouncing children. And as you who are reading this are probably an older rosy, bouncing child yourself, you know how great that is. Although your parents might not act it sometimes, you are really a treasure in your better moments, and they know it. Peninnah had children. And Hannah did not.

And the problem was, second, that Peninnah not only had rosy, bouncing children, but she also had a very, very nasty disposition. And one of her delights was to torment poor Hannah.

"What good are you?" she'd say. "You do not have children. What a waste! You are just taking up space." Which you will agree is no way to win friends and influence people. It's no way to keep peace in the family either.

Clearly, being on the sidelines can be pretty miserable business.

Does It Have to Be All Bad?

The trouble with having something wrong in our lives is that we often jump to the conclusion that *everything* is wrong.

"Everybody's against me."

"Nothing's going right."

"Everything's wrong."

"I can't think of one thing in my whole life that's going right."

Of course, this isn't so. It isn't so with you and it wasn't so with Hannah.

There was one bright spot with Hannah. Her husband Elkanah loved her very deeply. In fact he loved her more than he did Peninnah. Hannah was thankful enough for this, but always and everywhere, this one great sorrow was there, like a shadow over her life. She had no children.

Always it was worse when they went up to Shiloh to celebrate the Feast of Tabernacles.

The Feast of Tabernacles was like a holiday. It was a time of rejoicing, when people came to Shiloh to give thanks to God for their harvest. Whole families went. They all traveled to the feast together. They went in single families and they went in large groups with their neighbors. It was like one long picnic, the whole week of it. They ate under the open skies, and they slept in shelters that their fathers made of green branches and leaves with fruit hanging on them. If you wanted to, you could reach up and grab a bunch of grapes.

31

They brought thank offerings to the Tabernacle, to the brazen altar in the courtyard, and they stood and watched while one of the priests killed the animal they had brought. Part of it was an offering to God, part of it went to the priests. And then the family sat down to eat the rest. It was a happy feast of thanksgiving.

On the day that Elkanah presented his sacrifice, he would celebrate the occasion by giving presents. Now Peninnah got not only a present for herself, but presents for her children too. Hannah got only one present for herself, a bitter reminder that she was childless.

This is the way it was that day when our story opens.

The family had gathered around to eat.

Peninnah and her children were served first. She received her food with a smirk.[1] And Hannah struggled with the lump in her throat, trying to swallow around it. It was no use. She couldn't eat.

"Come, come, Hannah," said her husband. "Why aren't you eating? Why make such a fuss over having no children? Don't I give you more devotion and love than ten sons would?"

Hannah nodded gratefully to her husband. She looked at her plate. Then she looked at Peninnah. Auuuuuuuk.

It was no use. Nothing was ever going to get any better. Or was it?

Have You Tried God?

That was when she stumbled over to the Tabernacle and fell to her knees. "Oh, God," she said. She was moving her mouth with the words, but no sound came out. "You made the whole world. Surely you could send me a son. If you will look down on my sorrow and answer my prayer and give me a son, I—"

---

1. That's a mocking smile, a real nasty one. She had received her presents with a smirk too.

She stopped, breathing hard.

"I—why—I'll give him back to You!"

She never noticed Eli the priest who was sitting in the door of the Tabernacle. He was looking at her with a scowl as dark as a thundercloud.

"I'll dedicate him to You," she went on. "He can be Yours—he will serve You forever!"

There was a growl from the door of the Tabernacle.

"Must you come here to drink?" someone bellowed.

She nearly jumped out of her sandals.

It was the priest! It was the scowling priest! And what a rude thing to say!

Later, on her way back to her family shelter, she thought about it. She thought about Eli the priest's scolding and about her answers. But most of all she thought about what he had said at the end. "Cheer up! May the Lord of Israel grant you your petition, whatever it is!" And all her fear of him had melted at those words. He wasn't an old bear after all! And what he'd said had sounded like a—like a *prophecy*. Like it was actually going to happen! She was going to have a son!

Does God Really Care?

The next morning, the feeling was still with her. The family rose early and went back to the Tabernacle to worship. She looked at the place where she had knelt. She looked at Eli the priest. A long knowing look passed between them. Neither of them said a word.

But of one thing she was sure. God had heard her prayer. He knew about her problem. And He cared. She had never felt so close to God before.

But Does God Always Work It Out Your Way?

That depends on what you ask for. If you could answer that one, you'd be as smart as God. God is not Santa Claus, giving you every little thing you might want at the moment.

He will work it out *in a way that is best for you.*

The thing to remember is—that He cares about you and every little detail of your life. And you can depend on it—He makes no mistakes. He's never made a mistake yet, and He certainly isn't going to begin with you.

Sometimes What You Get Is What You Really Wanted

In Hannah's case, He did work it out her way. In no time at all, she was weaving cloth for little nighties and waiting for her child to be born. And you guessed it.

It was a boy.

She named him Samuel, and Samuel means, "Asked of God." And if anyone asked her, she said, "Well, I asked the Lord for him, didn't I?"

No matter how black things look, things do straighten out after awhile. And they did, for Hannah. Now Peninnah had nothing to smirk about. And now Peninnah's nasty disposition was entirely wasted on Hannah. Hannah was too busy and happy burping her baby to pay any attention.

When You Make a Promise
Do You Always Have to Keep It?

"As time goes by, don't circumstances change? And if everything is different than it was before—like with Hannah— when she promised to give that child back to God, do you really have to keep your promise? After all, she was desperate—but now she had this cuddly baby boy and all her problems were straightened out—and if God was so good to her in the first place, why should she have to part with the baby now, why would God make her do it—would she really have to—"

Oh, come *on* now. You're getting all tangled up in your own words. And you're fudging. And besides, you're missing the point.

The answer is yes, when you make a promise you're supposed to keep it, and yes, Hannah did keep her promise—not because she had to, but because she wanted to. She was pretty close to God, you see. And she knew that He was working everything out for her own good. And she knew for certain now, that He loved her and cared about her problems. And she knew that even if she gave up this child, God was still going to work out her life in a way that was best for her. So there was no longer anything to cry about.

God Loves a Promise-Keeper

She didn't give him up all at once, of course; he was too small. He had to be cared for. So for the next few years, Peninnah and the other children went up to Shiloh to the Feast of Tabernacles without her. She stayed home and took care of baby Samuel until he was old enough to get along without her care.

And then, the year he was ready, she packed his duds and went along with the rest of the family to Shiloh. They took along with them bullocks and some food for sacrifice. And they threw in a couple of extra bullocks as a present to Eli.

It was time to keep the promise. It was time to give Samuel back to God.

—Especially a CHEERFUL Promise-Keeper

Eli was bustling about the Tabernacle, giving orders to the lads who served him, and to his two sons who acted as priests. Well, bustling is hardly the word for it. Perhaps it's better to say that he *ambled*. For Eli couldn't bustle very well these days; he was older now, and his eyesight was poor. That's why he didn't recognize the man and woman and child when they came up to the door of the Tabernacle.

"Sir, you remember me?" the woman said. It was Hannah, of course.

He stared back at her blankly. He did not.

"Why I'm the woman who stood here that time, praying."

He still looked blank.

"And crying," she added. Ah, now, he was beginning to remember.

"Well, you didn't know what I was praying for. But I had asked God to give me this child."

Ah. Now his eyes lighted up.

"And He has given me my request," she said. "But I made a promise."

Promise?

"I made Him a promise that if He would give me a son, I would dedicate that son to Him. And this is what I am doing."

Eli looked at the boy again. What a fine strapping lad he was! Standing there straight and tall. Striking! Quite striking indeed! This was good news. Then Eli remembered his rudeness to the woman when she'd been there before. He had been quite boorish really, quite nasty. And now here she was back, presenting him with a fine lad to help him, to be like a son to him. He was getting better than he deserved. His old eyes twinkled and he smiled at Samuel again.

They all bowed their heads and worshiped God then and there. And thanked Him. And then the Tabernacle and the court and the countryside roundabout echoed with such rejoicing as people had not heard in years. It turned out that Hannah could sing and rejoice louder than she could cry. And better, too. It certainly made sweeter music.

It was a bright day in Shiloh. A bright day indeed!

Don't Knock the Sidelines

Yes, it's great to be right out there in first place, sailing through life in shining splendor, with everyone applauding. But it's not always too bad to be on the sidelines. God has wonderful things in store for people who stay on the sidelines too. For Hannah had a son who was dedicated to God, who was going places!

And that was better than going places herself!

The sidelines can be great—if that's where God wants you!

What About You?

When you make a promise, do you always keep it?

Write down the promises you've made—all you can think of.

Check off the ones you've kept. Are there one or two in there that you *haven't* kept? Do you suppose you could do a little road work and do something about keeping them?

So much for that. Now.

Do you feel that you're on the sidelines? If you are, don't stew about it.

"We share and share alike—those who go to the battle and those who guard the equipment" (1 Sam. 30:24, *TLB*).

I'VE GOT PLENTY OF TIME TO TRAIN

1 Samuel 3

All of Shiloh was asleep. The lights had been out for many hours. Everything was quiet, except for the nightbugs. The courtyard of the Tabernacle was quiet too, and dark. The big brazen altar where the sacrifices were made was like a huge shadow in the darkness. Between the altar and the Tabernacle was another shadow, this one smaller. It was the laver, filled with water, for the priests to wash their hands and feet before they went into the Tabernacle. Inside, the Tabernacle was dark, except for the light of the seven-lamp candlestick. It was always filled with just enough oil to last through the night. In the wee small hours before dawn, it had not gone out yet.

In an adjoining room in the court, the boy lay on his cot. He was sleeping soundly, his head turned upward. Everything was quiet, quiet—

When suddenly—

He stirred in his sleep, and then got up on one elbow.

What was that? It was a voice. He had heard a voice. Someone was calling him. It was no mistake. Whoever was calling him, was calling him by name. He sat up in bed.

The next moment he swung around, his feet on the floor. And the *next* moment he was groping his way out of the room in the dim light.

"But Why Should I Have to Train Now?"

"I'm going to be a great man some day. After all, I have good parents, I'm getting a good education, I have all kinds of chances. My dad tells me I have more opportunities than lots of kids do. My dad says too, that you have to be in the right place at the right time. And I *plan* to be in the right place at the right time. When the time comes, I'm going to be somebody, believe me. And when I get older, I'm going to start getting ready for it. Uh—what's that? What am I doing now? Well I'm—uh—just sort of fooling around. Actually there isn't much I can do now—that is, there isn't anything important or exciting."

News for you. Training and practicing is never exciting when you're young. Or when you get older either. Practicing can be a bore and training can be dull. Doing the same thing over and over again can be tiresome. And obeying isn't always easy either. Especially when you'd rather be doing *this* when you're supposed to be doing *that*.

"You Are Now Becoming What You Are Going to Be"

Think about that for a minute. You're not just standing still, you know. Every day you're a day older. And with everything you do and every decision you make, you are *becoming the person you are going to be.* So it sure pays to get an early start. Samuel got an early start.

"What? Chores? To Be Great I Have to Do Chores?"

The Tabernacle might have been the house of God, but it was still run by *men.*

The Tabernacle was in a large court about the size of one-and-a-half city lots. The great brazen altar was there for the sacrifices. It had to be kept clean and polished, and the ashes had to be carried away. The huge brazen laver was there. It had to be kept filled with water.

The Tabernacle itself had to be kept clean. It was divided into two rooms. The large one was called the holy place and only the priests went in there. The second room was the most sacred place in the Tabernacle—it was called the holy of holies. And only the high priest was ever allowed to go in there, and he was allowed to go in only once a year.

There was just one piece of furniture in there—the ark of the covenant. It was the sacred ark of God. You read about it in the story of Joshua. And you'll hear more about it in the next chapter.

And then there were the doors that had been added to the Tabernacle to make it more beautiful. They had to be opened each morning and closed each evening. And the lamps had to be filled with oil. They had to be lighted at night.

And then there were studies. Ughhhh.

Yes—studies too.

There were servants there, but Samuel had to do his share of work.

It was Eli whom Samuel followed around. It was Eli who watched over him. It was Eli who needed him too. For the old priest was nearly blind by now.

"Work? When Others Are Goofing Off?"

"It's easy to work and behave yourself when everybody else is doing it. Because then you're just going along with the gang. But when everybody's goofing off but you—it makes you feel sort of odd, being the only good guy in the whole place—sort of lonely. If I were in Samuel's shoes, I could be good, too. It's different with me than it was with Samuel. I'm in school where lots of the kids *aren't* behaving. And they *do* goof off. After all, Samuel was working in the house of the Lord. It was easy for him. He had a better time of it than I do."

Not so, not so. If anything, he had a *worse* time of it. For Samuel had to toe the mark while others all around him were goofing off. What? In the house of the Lord? Yes, in the house of the Lord. And what's more, the "others" were two of Eli's own sons!

"I Hate Guys Who Say 'Me First!' "

Now if you ran into somebody who always said, "Me first—I want the best part—and all I can get"—you would know that you were up against a real rascal. Anybody who lives by that set of rules has got to be bad news.

And let's face it—Eli's sons were bad news. They were in charge when people came with their animals to offer sacrifices. They took part of the meat first, before the animal had been placed on the altar as an offering to God. And they took the *best* part for themselves. And they took more than was rightfully theirs.

Now this "me first—the best part—and all I can get" didn't go over so well with the people who came to worship. "Take as much as you want!" they cried, "but the fat must first be burned for the Lord as the law requires!"

"No way!" they'd say. "Give it to us now, or we'll take it by force!" The Bible tells us: *So the sin of these young men was very great in the eyes of the Lord, for they treated the people's offerings to the Lord with contempt.*[1]

Well, DO You Goof Off Because Everyone Else Does?

No you don't. You keep plugging on, just as Samuel did. Eli's wicked sons were doing what they wanted to. And Samuel was doing what *he* wanted to. He wanted to obey God. And it was a good life. It was terrific! He was growing like mad

1. 1 Samuel 2:17, *TLB*.

in two ways. He was getting taller and bigger. But he was also getting brighter, and more popular with everyone. And the Bible tells us that he was a favorite of the Lord's.

It was exciting to grow taller and stronger and smarter. It was exciting to develop brain and muscles. There were hours spent with old Eli—listening, reading, writing. There were hours of play out in the bright sunshine too. But the most exciting times of the years were the holidays—especially the week of the Feast of Tabernacles—the harvest feast.

People came from all over the country to build their booths and offer their sacrifices and sing and worship the Lord—and to enjoy each other.

And was Samuel ever busy! He carried jars of fresh water and did errands and waited on Eli—and watched the travelers eagerly, until finally he'd see those familiar faces—his father and mother and the rest of his family—and he would nearly jump out of his skin.

"Samuel, Samuel!" his mother would cry. "Oh, my son, my son!" And then her words would come out fast, tumbling over each other—"Have you been a good boy? Of course, you—Oh, how splendid you look—how you've grown! Samuel! You're getting lots of sunshine. Your cheeks are tan. Have you learned much? You're getting so *tall!*" And on and on it would go, until they were all laughing and crying together. And then, out it would come from her luggage!

"A coat! Mother—mother, it's handsome!" Samuel would cry. "May I try it on?"

"Of course you may try it on. Ah. So. There. See how it fits! Just perfectly! I made it bigger this year, all around!"

Yes, always there was a coat. She wove it with her nimble fingers, and she wove into it her love. And every year it was bigger. And every year she would cry, "Samuel, you are such a big boy!" And she would hug him.

And then there was the year when the coat came out, and he said, "Thank you, mother. It's handsome. May I try it

43

on?" But he said it with a little more dignity. And he tried it on, and he thanked her. But she did not hug him; he was getting too big to hug. At least in front of people.

Yes, time was flying. And Samuel was growing up.

Every year it was a little easier to see his family go back home again. For every year he was getting more and more used to staying at the Tabernacle. It was home. And Eli was like a father to him.

Some Goofer-Offers Wake Up Too Late

Eli was getting used to Samuel too. Samuel was more like a son to him than his own sons were. He did his best to make his own sons obey. "I've been hearing terrible reports about what you are doing," he'd grumble to them. "It's bad enough when you sin against other people. But you've been sinning against the Lord. Why don't you shape up?" But they wouldn't listen. Eli was doing the right thing in trying to get them to obey, but he was doing the right thing too late. For the time to teach them to obey was when they were young, and he had never done it.[2]

There's Trouble Ahead!

God had given Eli the job of being the high priest in the Tabernacle. But one of the most important jobs He had given Eli was to teach his own sons to obey so they could take up the priesthood when he was gone. But he hadn't done it, and now everything was in a mess. There could be nothing but trouble ahead. Things could only go from bad to worse.

One day a prophet came to Eli and gave him a message from the Lord. And what was the message? You guessed it. Things *were* going to go from bad to worse. Which brings us up to that unforgettable night when Samuel heard the voice.

2. If your parents are making you obey, don't squirm too hard; they're doing you a favor.

Is God Really Talking to Me?

Yes—the boy in the bed was Samuel.

"It must be Eli," he thought as he groped his way out of his room and went to where Eli was sleeping. "Here I am, Eli," he said. "What do you want?"

"Ummmmmphgrummmmph—what? That you, Samuel? What do you want?" Eli struggled awake.

"You called me. I came to find out—what do *you* want?"

Eli blinked his nearly blind eyes. "I didn't call you," he whispered. "Go back to bed."

Samuel groped his way back to his cot and settled down. That was strange. Was it a dream? It must have been a—

Wait a minute.

There it was again. "Samuel," the voice said. There was no mistaking it.

And again—"Samuel."

Samuel was wide awake now. He jumped up with a start, and ran back to Eli. "Yes?" he said. "What do you need?"

Eli hadn't gone back to sleep. "No, I didn't call you, my son," he said. "Go on—back to bed. Away with you."

Samuel went slowly back to his cot. He didn't know what to make of it. By now he could see well in the dark.

He'd barely got back in his bed when he heard it again. "Samuel."

Samuel scrambled out of bed and was gone like a shot out of a gun—back to Eli's cot. "Yes!" he said again. "What do you need, Eli?"

This time, Eli got up on his elbows and stared through the dim light at Samuel. There was a long silence as the truth dawned on him. "Samuel," he said, and his voice was trembling. "Go back to your cot and lie down again."

"Yes, Eli."

"And if He calls again, say to Him—'Yes, Lord, I'm listening.'"

What? *What?* Yes, *Lord?* Why this was unbelievable! Samuel had never been on speaking terms with God before. He went slowly back to his cot. He was trembling. He lay there in the dark, waiting. And listening. And waiting. Perhaps it had only been a dream. Perhaps he'd been mistaken after all. Perhaps—

"Samuel."

Samuel's scalp prickled. There it was again. And this time the Lord was standing there!

He hadn't been dreaming. It was no mistake. But was it, could it really be the Lord? Samuel couldn't quite believe it. "Yes—" he began, but he didn't say yes, *Lord.* Just, "Yes. I'm listening." Would the Lord speak to him? Would He say more? Samuel waited, holding his breath.

"I am going to do a shocking thing in Israel," the Lord said, "I am going to do all the things the prophet warned Eli about." Samuel listened, wide-eyed. "I've continually threatened him and his family with punishment because his sons are wicked and he doesn't stop them." And the Lord went on to tell Samuel what the punishment was to be. And the punishment was so dreadful that Samuel's heart almost stopped beating just hearing about it.

Long after the Lord had gone, Samuel lay there in the dark, hardly daring to move. He had never known God before, or heard Him speak. This was shocking. This was unbelievable!

At last the oil was gone in the lamps. They flickered and went out. And then the first streaks of dawn began to creep into the room.

Now came the worst part. Now he would have to tell Eli, whom he loved.

This Job Isn't Going to Be Easy

But he didn't want to tell Eli. He bustled about, doing his chores, opening the doors of the Tabernacle, emptying ashes, cleaning and filling lamps—

At last he could put it off no longer. Eli called him. "My son," he said, "what did the Lord say to you?"

46

Samuel dug the toe of his sandal into the ground, made a mark, stared at it.

"Tell me everything," Eli said, quietly, "and may God punish you if you hide anything from me." Well that was it. It was an order.

Samuel obeyed the hardest order that he'd ever had to obey in his life. He told Eli what the Lord had said. They stood there for a long while, not saying anything. Then, "It's the Lord's will," Eli said finally, "let Him do what He thinks best." He walked away.

Samuel stood there for a long minute, and then roused himself and went to fetch water for the laver in the Tabernacle.

Me? A Hero?

Things went on as they had before. Nothing happened. Samuel kept on learning, and the Lord was with him, and gave him wisdom.

And then a strange thing began to happen. The people began to listen carefully to his advice. They listened to everything he said. And they passed the word on. And before he knew it, Samuel became famous! The Bible says, *All Israel, from Dan to Beersheba knew that Samuel was going to be a prophet of the Lord.* That's like saying, "Everyone knew, from Maine to California."

Then the Lord began to give messages to him there at the Tabernacle, and he passed them on to the people of Israel.

He was a national hero!

Samuel had been training and obeying and working at it all his life. And now at last he had come into his own. At last he had arrived. But what about the prophecy the Lord had given him that night? The prophecy about Eli? And his sons?

THERE WAS DOOM AHEAD. But God had raised Himself up a prophet who was going to be equal to the task. And that prophet was Samuel.

What About You?

Can you think of opportunities that you've missed because you weren't ready?

Why weren't you ready?

Check the right answers. And don't fudge.

1. I was goofing off.
2. I didn't want to practice.
3. Training was a bore.
4. I was just lazy.
5. I figured there was plenty of time.

What could you have done to be ready? Is it too late to do it now? It isn't too late—get going.

"Yes, remember your Creator now while you are young . . ." (Eccl. 12:6, *TLB*).

IS GOD TRYING TO TELL US SOMETHING?

1 Samuel 4—6

Shiloh was in shambles.

Most of the fighting men had gone off to war, and the people who were left were in complete and total confusion. They were waiting for news of the battle.

Eli sat in his seat at the city gate. His hands trembled. And his heart was trembling too. He was ninety-eight years old now, and blind. His days of power and as the head of the priesthood were a thing of the past. He was now just a very frightened old man.

An embattled soldier came scrambling up the hill toward the city. His clothes were torn and there was dirt on his head—a sign of mourning. He stumbled through the city gates, and went past the old man sitting there. He went into the broad place inside the city gates, where the crowds were.

There he delivered his message and dropped with exhaustion. And a great wail went up from the people.

When the old man heard it, he started up from his perch, and then sank back again. He was too old and too fat to move fast anymore. "What is it?" he cried out. "What is it?" But there was no one to hear or pay him any attention. "What is the noise all about?" And the messenger turned to him. "I have just come home from the battle," he said. "Yes!" cried Eli. "Yes, yes! What happened?" And the messenger gave him the news. It was bad—worse than anything Eli had expected. It was so bad that it literally knocked him over backwards. And he fell from his perch with a great groan. The worst had happened. Shiloh was doomed. All Israel was doomed. Everything that Samuel had predicted had come true!

How Could This Thing Happen?

It had come about gradually and in a roundabout way. And of course it started with the Philistines. It always started with the Philistines.

They had been nipping and nibbling at the Israelites for years—taking little bites here and there, and keeping all Israel in a state of uproar. The real trouble started when they decided they'd had enough nipping, and would finish the job once and for all. They decided they would wipe Israel off the face of the earth.

And they nearly did it, too. It was a terrible battle—one of the biggest they'd had in years. It was an all-out attack on the part of the Philistines and an all-out defense for the Israelites. And what happened?

Well, the Philistines made mincemeat out of the Israelites is what happened. They all but finished them off. Four thousand of their soldiers were killed.

They went crawling back to their cities, their tails between their legs, like whipped dogs. They didn't have a chance.

"What can we do?" they wailed. And, "We don't have a chance!" they cried. "They have a trained army. They have chariots! If we don't do something quick they'll *pulverize*[1] us!"

And the leaders got together to hash over what had happened—and what they were going to do about it.

"Is God Trying to Tell Us Something?"

This is the first question they should have asked themselves. For years they'd been turning their backs on God. Most of them had turned to worshiping idols. It had been a long time since they'd cared whether God was trying to tell them anything at all. There were only a few of them left who were still worshiping God and only a few stragglers came to Shiloh anymore. And even on the holy feast days when they were all supposed to go to Shiloh to worship God, the traffic wasn't very heavy—at least they didn't have any traffic jams. The truth was, that God *was* trying to tell them something. But they weren't listening. They were too busy scheming their own schemes. And this time, they outschemed themselves.

Is Believing God Like Having a Magic Wand?

No. And God isn't a fairy godmother. And He isn't Santa Claus. And He isn't a "good-luck" charm. He is *the* holy God who made the universe. And His holiness and His power do not rest in *things*. This is where the leaders who were scheming made their mistake.

"The Ark!" they cried. "That's it—the Ark! If we take the Ark into battle with us, we'll have it made!"

The *Ark!?!*

Why, the Ark was the beautiful golden box that Moses had been commanded to build—that had gone everywhere with the Israelites in their wanderings. But once they were settled in the Promised Land that God had given them, the Ark was to be kept in the holiest place in the Tabernacle at Shiloh. And it was supposed to *stay* in there. Only the

1. Scrunch us down to dust.

high priest was ever allowed to see it, and then only once a year. It had inside it, Aaron's rod that budded and a pot of the manna the Israelites had eaten in the wilderness, and the Ten Commandments God had given to Moses. The Ark stood for the presence of God. It wasn't a "good-luck" charm. Had they lost their minds?

Don't Do It—Don't Do It!

It was the stupidest thing they could have done. It was like pulling a loose piece of yarn in a sweater, and pulling it and pulling it. Once you start pulling, the thing gets worse and worse until the sweater comes apart completely. By taking that Ark out of its holy place, they were pulling that piece of yarn and Israel was about to come unraveled completely. Would they do it?

"The Ark!" they cried. "Get the Ark!"

Oh, *no!*

"Get the Ark out of the Tabernacle in Shiloh. We'll carry it with us into battle. Then we can't lose!"

"How shall we get it? Who will get it for us?"

"Eli would never consent to it."

"Or Samuel."

"Eli's sons! Ask them! They'll let us have it!"

This is exactly what they decided to do. They were tugging at the yarn.

Oh, NO!

A little party of men was sent to go fetch the Ark.

When they came to get it, Eli fussed and fumed and raged in vain. He had never made his sons obey when they were boys; they were not about to obey him now. He was pushed aside, an old man with no authority. And Samuel was too young to have any say about it at all.

And they put the poles through the gold rings in the Ark and—hup!—hoisted it up on their shoulders. And off they went, Eli's sons with them, leaving a trembling Eli behind.

It's Working, It's Working!

When the Israelite army saw the Ark coming into their camp—

"The Ark! The Ark!"

"They've got it!"

"One look at that Ark and the Philistines will scatter in all directions!"

"We'll never be bothered with them again!" And they jumped up and down and hugged each other for joy. And the noise rose to the skies.

"THE ARK!!!" They could be heard for miles.

And that was the trouble.

Good grief.

Yes. The Philistines had heard it too.

The Scheme That Worked Too Well

"What's this?" the Philistines cried. "What's the meaning of all this noise?"

"What's going on?"

"What are they shouting about in the camp of the Israelites?"

And when they found out it was because the Ark of the Lord had arrived, they *panicked.*

"They've got God in their camp!" they cried.

"Woe upon us!"

"We've never had to face anything like this before!"

"Why that's the God who destroyed the Egyptians with plagues!"

"And parted the Red Sea!"

But did the Philistines run?

Oh, if they only had!

But they did not.

The scheme was working all right—it was working too well.

The Philistines decided that if they were number two—they'd better try harder.

"Fight as you've never fought before!" they rallied. "Or we'll all become their slaves, just as they've been *our* slaves!"

It was a fearful battle. It was PANDEMONIUM.[2]

The Philistines had fought before with the fierceness of anger and cruelty. But now they fought with the fierceness of *terror.*

There was hardly anyone left in the Israelite army to tell the tale. And then—

Oh, *no.* The worst possible thing had happened.

The Ark! THE ARK!!

And that's when one of the soldiers broke loose from the battlefield and ran toward Shiloh.

The Doom Is Here

The soldier staggered up the hill, half dead with fright and exhaustion. He stumbled in the gate, his clothes torn and dirt on his head.[3] He was so crazed with grief and fear that he didn't see old Eli sitting at the gate until he heard him cry, "What's the matter? What's all this noise about?"

He rushed over to the old man who was sitting on his perch, frightened and trembling. "I've just come from the battle," he said.

"How did it go, my son?" the old man said. "Tell me quickly."

And the messenger began his tragic report.

"Israel has fled from before the Philistines."

"Fled?"

"There's also been a great slaughter among our people. And that's not all."

"And?"

"Your two sons—are dead."

The old man clutched the sides of his perch for support.

---

2. An uproar. Not an ordinary uproar, an absolutely wild uproar. Good word!
3. A sign of great grief and mourning.

He was trembling all over. He did not dare to ask the next question. He didn't have to.

"Yes," the messenger said. "They've captured the Ark—the holy Ark of God is gone."

The old man's hands flew to his heart, and he gasped for breath. And he rolled over backward, off his perch. And he landed with a great sickening thud on the ground behind him.

The people ran around to pick him up. They leaned over him for a moment. Then one of them stood up slowly. "It's no use," he said. "He's dead. He broke his neck when he fell."

And the Bible tells us he was an old man, and heavy—*and he had judged Israel forty years.*

But now he was gone, and his two sons were gone—and there was only Samuel left to carry on the task.

The terrible doom that Samuel had told Eli about, had come to pass.

But what of the holy Ark of God?

Where did it go?

And what would happen to it now?

The Gloom After the Doom

Well, the Philistines thought that the Ark was a magic box. They thought they had a magic idol. They were delighted. Where should they take it? Well, where else, but to the house of *their* chief god—the house of Dagon! Put the two gods together! What else indeed?

And this is exactly what they did.

Now we know that that was a presumptuous[4] thing to do. It was absolutely unthinkable. It could lead to nothing but trouble. The Philistines didn't know it yet.

But they soon found out.

4. Real smart-alecky.

For the very next morning they opened the door of their temple to go in, and—

The Ark was exactly as they had left it the night before. But their idol Dagon—

It had fallen smack on its face and was sprawled on the ground in front of the Ark! And it looked for all the world as if it were face down before the Ark of God!

Carefully they lifted their idol up and set it back in its place. So now everything would be all right.

What's This?

The next morning when they opened the doors of the temple—

Auuuuugh!

The idol of Dagon had fallen down again before the Ark of God! And this time his head had broken off. And his hands had broken off. And they lay on the threshold in the entrance to the temple!

And this time it was not only the idol of Dagon that got clobbered—it was the people too. For up one street and down the other and all over the city of Ashdod, the people had boils! And most of their crops were destroyed by a plague of mice!

Well, before you could say "Dagon," the leaders had called a meeting. And the motion was made and carried—"We'll all perish along with our god Dagon! Get the Ark out of here! Let it be carried to the city of Gad! Perhaps things will be better in Gad."

And What's THIS?

But they weren't.
"Plague!!!"
Auuugh!
"Get it out of here! Take it to Ekron! Maybe things will be better there!"

And What's THIS?

But they weren't.

While the Philistines were still coming down the road toward Ekron with the Ark, and when the people of Ekron saw it coming, they were already screaming so loud the noise reached the sky. "DON'T BRING IT IN HERE!" they screamed, and, "THEY'RE BRINGING THE ARK HERE TO KILL US TOO!" they bellowed.

You guessed it. A plague had already begun, and fear was sweeping the city. The Bible tells us that those who didn't die were deathly ill, and there was weeping everywhere.

The whole city dissolved in one great cry for help.

And this time nobody suggested sending the Ark to another city; nobody dared to. In the end the Philistines decided to get rid of it altogether.

How?

Give it back to the Israelites!

"We Don't Want It
You Can Have It It's Too Much for Us! ! !"

They sent for their wise men, and their magicians to tell them what to do in this terrible calamity. Their wise men and magicians got in a huddle and pulled their beards. "Send it back," they said finally. "But don't send it back in an ordinary way. And don't send it back empty. Make models of the tumors caused by the plague. And make models of the mice that ate up our crops. Make five of them, one for each of their cities. Put them in a little box."

"But how shall we send it back? Who'll take it?"

"Prepare a new cart," the wise men said, "and fasten the cart to two milk cows that have never been harnessed before. Put the Ark of God on the cart. And the little box with the golden models."

"But what about the calves that belong to the two cows?"

"AhHAH. That's just the point. That's where the trick comes in. Lock up the calves in the barn. And let the cows go—let them pull the cart wherever they wish. If they go to the land of Israel, then we'll know that it's the Israelites' God who has sent this evil upon us. But if they go toward the barn to be with their calves, then we'll know the whole thing was just a coincidence."[5]

Phew! At Last!

So they prepared the new cart, hitched up the cows, locked up the calves—and—

The cows marched straight down the road in the opposite direction toward the land of Israel, mooing as they went. And the Philistine leaders followed them as far as the border of the village called Beth-Shemesh.

The farmers of Beth-Shemesh were out in their fields reaping wheat, when one of them heard some mooing. He looked up and saw—

Two cows coming, dragging a cart behind them, and on the cart was—

The Ark of God!

They went absolutely wild with joy.

People came running from all directions, as the cows pulled the cart on until they came to the field of a man named Joshua.[6] And there they stopped by a large rock. Nobody had told them where to go or where to stop. They just seemed to know.

Imagine getting the precious Ark back! It was almost too good to be true.

They broke up the wood from the cart, and killed the cows, and sacrificed them to the Lord as a burnt offering. Then several priests from the tribe of Levi lifted the Ark, and the chests that had the golden offerings in them and laid them on the rock. After the five Philistine leaders, who had followed

5. They'd know that the evil just "happened to happen" at the same time the Ark was in the towns—that they really didn't have anything to do with each other.
6. This is not the walls-of-Jericho Joshua.

the cows, watched for a while, they went back home, glad
to be rid of the whole business.

Only a Box?

But there were some of the Israelites who didn't seem to
be able to leave well enough alone. There are a few in every
crowd. There were a few in this one. They stared at the Ark
with idle curiosity as if it were a float in a parade instead
of the holy Ark of God. They walked around it and they
snooped at it and they touched it and they *opened it and
looked inside.*

Why even the priests were not allowed to do such a thing.

Death was the punishment?

Death was the punishment.

The Bible says that these men died.

No—The Holy Ark of God

The men of Shemesh were frightened.

"Who is able to stand before this holy God?" they cried.
"Where can we send it from here?" And they sent messengers
to the village of Kiriath-jearim: "The Philistines have sent
the Ark back!" they cried, and in the next breath—"Take
it away! Get it out of here!"

So the men of Kiriath-jearim came and took the Ark to
the hillside home of a chap named Abinadab. And they
installed his son Eleazar to be in charge of it.

Clearly, the holy Ark of God was not to be trifled with.

—And You'd Better Believe It

For twenty-nine years, the Ark stayed there. They never
took it back to Shiloh. For Shiloh had been sacked and the
Tabernacle destroyed. Eli was gone. And all their hopes and
dreams were gone. For it seemed that the Lord had abandoned
them. For so many years they hadn't wanted Him; now He
had left them alone.

These were sad dark days for Israel.

This was the doom that followed the gloom.

But What of Samuel?
Oh, he was around all right—very much around. He had not deserted God. And God had not deserted him.

He'll pop up again. Wait and see.

What About You?
The Ark was something to remind the people that God was with them. He never said He was *in* it. To the Israelites, the Ark became a magic *thing*. And the idea grew on them, until they thought more of the *thing* than they did of God.

God isn't a Fairy Godmother.

Or a magic wand.

Or Santa Claus.

He is *the* holy God who made the world. And His holiness and power do not rest in things.

Are you putting your faith in things?

Like carrying your Bible (*carrying* it, that is—not *reading* it).

Wearing a cross on a chain.

Or wearing a "religious" medal.

Or praying pat little prayers that you've repeated so often you can say them backwards with your tongue tied behind your back.

There's nothing wrong with any of these things. It's just that they are not *enough*. God makes it very plain: "I am the Lord! That is my name, and I will not give my glory to anyone else; I will not share my praise with carved idols" (Isa. 42:8, *TLB*).

The Ark wasn't enough for the Israelites. And even good things are not enough for us.

And Paul tells us: "I have given up everything else—I have found it to be the only way to really know Christ . . ." (Phil. 3:10, *TLB*).

Yes. He wants you to know Him. *Personally.*

WE WANT
TO MAKE OUR
OWN RULES
1 Samuel 8—10

"We want one too!"
"Everyone else has one!"
"We want to be like everyone else!"
"We want to make the rules of the game!"

What sort of nonsense was this? Who were these people? And what was it they wanted?

Well, these people were the Israelites, and they wanted to change the rules of the game. And they wanted a new coach.

But Why?

Although Shiloh was in shambles and there was no longer a central place of worship—actually the Israelites were doing very well. They had been doing pretty well for many years.

The people couldn't come to Shiloh? All right—so Samuel

took Shiloh to the people. He became a traveling preacher—a sort of an early-day circuit-rider, holding court, advising the people on spiritual matters—and legal matters too.

"If you are serious about wanting to return to the Lord," he would cry, "get rid of your foreign gods and your idols!" And they did! And sure enough, their enemies began to leave them more or less alone. Some of their cities were returned. They had their ups and downs, but in general, there was peace.

What's the Problem?

Samuel's home was in Ramah. There he lived with his wife and two sons and there he built an altar to the Lord. And though he was a judge in Ramah, it was only his stopping place for he was traveling most of the time. He preached and the people listened and he taught and the people learned. And everything was going so well, it looked as if they'd live happily ever after. And then—

Samuel appointed his two sons to assist him in his duties. He gave them the southern district to take care of, while he kept the northern district for himself. And that's where the trouble began. For while Samuel was a good leader, his sons, sad to say, were not.

They were sneaky, they were greedy, and they accepted bribes. In other words they were dishonest and crooked rascals.

Hold It—Hold It!

So the leaders of Israel got together and went up to Samuel's hometown. "Since you went into semi-retirement,"[1] they said, "things haven't been too good. We don't like to come right out and say it, but your sons are a couple of underhanded rascals." And before Samuel had a chance to say "Come let us reason together," they set up this clamor about changing all the rules of the game.

---

1. That's sort of like working only half-time.

"Give us a king!" they whined, "like all the other nations have." And, "We need a strong leader in war," they whimpered, "to help us fight our enemies!"[2] And, "We're the only nation that doesn't have a king!" they sulked, "and we want one."

What?

They wanted a strong *leader?* Why *God* had been their leader ever since He'd led them out of Egypt! Other nations just had kings; they had GOD. This was what had always made them different from all other nations. What were they talking about? Had they lost their heads?

They had lost their heads.

Samuel couldn't believe his poor old ears. To say he was astonished is putting it mildly. He was absolutely thunderstruck.

Don't Chuck Out the Rules

Why, ever since that night God had called Samuel in the dim light of his room at the Tabernacle, he had known he was going to be the spiritual leader of Israel. All his boyhood he had trained for it. And all through the rest of his life he had lived it. These people were not just part of his life. These people *were* his life. And now they were throwing him over like a gunnysack full of old shoes. They wanted new rules for the game. They wanted a new coach.

You May Be Chucking the Rule-Maker

Now the Israelites might not have known where to go when they needed advice. But Samuel did. He went to God.

"God," he cried, "these people are throwing me out. All my life I've worked for them. And now they're throwing me out like an old reject. I know I'm old, but I'm not finished. Whatever shall I do?"

---

2. Yes, their old enemies the Philistines and the Ammonites were getting nippy again.

"Don't be so upset, Samuel," said God. "They're not reject- ing you—they're rejecting *Me*. I have been their God ever since I led them out of Egypt. I was their God all through the wilderness. I was their God when they crossed the Jordan and came into this land. And they've been throwing Me aside practically every step of the way. And now they're giving you the same treatment."

"Whatever shall I do?" Samuel said again.

"Tell them they can have their king," said God.

What?

"But it'll mean nothing but trouble!" said Samuel. "Do they realize what they're in for?"

"Tell them what they're in for," said God. "And don't pull any punches."

You Can Have Your Own Way—BUT

Samuel did. And he didn't pull any punches either. "If you insist upon having a king," he said, "this is what it will be like. Your sons will be inducted into the army. A king will make them run before his chariot. Some of your sons will lead his troops into battle."

"We don't care!"

"Others will be slave-labor. They'll be forced to plow in the king's royal fields and harvest his crops without pay."

"That's all right!"

"They'll be forced to make his weapons and his chariot equipment. And your daughters too. He'll take them from you and force them to cook and bake and make perfumes for him."

"Let him, let him!"

"He'll take away the best of your fields and vineyards and olive groves and give them to his friends. He'll take a tenth of your harvest and pass it out among his favorites."

"Okay—okay!"

"He'll use your animals for his personal gain!"

"We don't care!"

"You'll have to pay taxes. He'll demand a tenth of your flocks and you'll be his slaves!"

"Give us a king!"

Don't Say You Weren't Warned

Samuel sighed. "You will shed bitter tears because of this king you are demanding. And the Lord will not help you. And you can't excuse yourselves on the grounds that you acted without knowledge."

And he sighed again.

And after they'd heard all the things that would happen to them if they insisted on having a king—did they say they'd changed their minds?

No.

"Even so—" they bellowed—"WE WANT A KINNNNNNNGGGG!!!!"

Do You Have to Be Hit over the Head Before You'll Listen?

Samuel threw up his hands in despair.

"Lord?" he said.

"Yes."

"Did you hear what these people *said?*"

"Yes."

"So?"

"So tell them they can have a king. They're going to have to learn the hard way."

Samuel sighed—a long one this time. This was like coming to the end of one chapter and beginning another. "Go back to your cities and wait," he told the men. "I'll keep in touch with you." Nothing would ever be the same again, he thought . . .

And nothing ever was.

So You're Going to Learn the Hard Way

The people of Israel got just what they wanted. They

changed the rules to suit themselves. And after they got their own way, were they happy?

Blaahhhh.

What happened next changed the whole history of Israel.

It changed the life of a young man who lived in the city of Gibeah too. He didn't know it, but his life was about to be turned upside down. His name was Saul.

More about him in the next chapter.

What About You?

Did you ever want to throw out all the rules and make up your own? Did you ever want something you really shouldn't have? But you clamored and stewed and whined until you got it anyway?

Well, what happened? Did you whine after you got it?

Do you have something right now that you shouldn't have, because you whined for it? If you do, it would be smart to drop it like a hot potato. If you're even *thinking* about something you want that you shouldn't have—drop the *idea* like a hot potato.

If you don't, you might have to learn the hard way.

"I have set the Lord always before me: because he is at my right hand, I shall not be moved (Ps. 16:8, *KJV*).

OFF TO A GOOD START

1 Samuel 9—10

It started out like any ordinary day. When Saul got up that morning, there wasn't a clue that this day was going to be different than any other. He had no idea that before the day was over, his whole life would be turned upside down.

It started out in the most ordinary way. Some of his father's donkeys strayed away. Now his father was very rich and influential in the little town of Gibeah and his donkeys were some of his most valuable possessions. And it was important that they be found. And so Saul and his servant started out to look for them. It doesn't seem possible that anything exciting could come from that. But something exciting did.

Is Any Day Really Ordinary?

The search for the donkeys turned out to be quite a hike. Saul and his servant went on and on and *on*. They traveled

73

through all the hill country of Ephraim, and into the land of Shalishah—their little trip began to look like a cross-country marathon. On and on they went, into the Shaalim area. Before they finished, they had covered the entire land of Benjamin. And couldn't find the donkeys anywhere.

Everywhere they went they asked if people had seen the donkeys. And everywhere they went people stared at Saul. Why? Because Saul was so tall and so handsome that he could have started a health spa. The Bible tells us he was head and shoulders above all other men. Saul was just a man people looked at twice.

On and on they went until they finally got to the land of Zuph. Saul looked at his servant. "Phew!" he said, "Enough! Let's go home. By now my father will be more worried about us than about the donkeys."

"Wait," said the servant. "I just thought of something. We're almost at Ramah. D'you know there's a prophet who lives in Ramah?"

"A prophet?"

"He's held in high honor by all the people. Everything he says comes true. Let's go and find him. Maybe he can tell us where the donkeys are."

The first thing Saul thought about was money. "We don't have any money to pay him with," he said. "Even our food is gone. We don't have a thing to give him." The servant thought a minute. "I have a quarter of a shekel of silver,"[1] he said. "It isn't much, but we can offer it to him. We can't lose. The worst he can do is say no."

"Yes indeed. What do we have to lose? Let's go," said Saul. And they started toward Ramah.

As they were climbing the hill toward the city, they saw some young girls coming down to draw water. "Do you know if there's a prophet in the town?" they asked. And the girls all began to talk at once.

1. A dollar.

"Yes. Stay right on this road."

"He lives just inside the city gates."

"He just came back from a trip."

"That's right. He's going to take part in a public sacrifice up on the hill."

"You'd better hurry."

"Yes, you'd better hurry. He'll probably be leaving about the time you get there."

"Yes, he has to arrive to bless the food."

Well, what a lot of chatterboxes *they* were.

But then Saul was such an impressive stately figure, looking down at them from his lofty heights, they lost their heads and tripped over their tongues. He was like a Redwood tree in the midst of a bunch of saplings. Ordinarily the girls of those times didn't chatter like that with total strangers. But you can see at once when people talked with tall Saul, they realized at once that they were not talking to an ordinary person.

You Never Know Whom You'll Run Into

Anyhow Saul and his servant thanked them and went on into the city. And just as they were going into the city gates they saw a man coming toward them. He was an old man. There was nothing special about him—except his eyes. His eyes seemed to burn right through them. "Excuse me, sir," Saul said, "but can you tell us where the prophet's house is?"

The old man stared at him a minute. "I am the prophet," he said quietly. "I am Samuel."

What? This old man—Samuel?

Or What Will Happen

"You'll come with me to the sacrificial feast," the old man went on. "And in the morning I'll tell you what you want to know and send you on your way."

What? This was Samuel—*the* famous Samuel—the one and

only Samuel? And he was inviting Saul to his feast? To the sacrificial feast? And all Saul had been thinking about was his donkeys! This was too much!

The prophet Samuel went on as if he could read Saul's mind. "Oh," he said, "and don't worry about those donkeys that were lost three days ago. They've been found. And anyway, *the desire of all Israel is on you,* you know. You have more to think about now than donkeys."

Oh, *that* was it. The prophet had made a mistake. "Pardon me, sir," Saul said. "I'm from the tribe of Benjamin, the smallest in Israel. And of all the families in the tribe, my family is the least important. I'm so sorry, sir. You have the wrong man."

What Is God Up To?

By this time, they had reached the place of the feast. Saul's head was whirling. This prophet had made a mistake. "Right here," the prophet was saying, as he directed Saul to the chief place. Right where the VIP's sat! Saul's eyes boggled in his head. How did this prophet know about his father's donkeys? How did this prophet know who he was?

"Bring this man the choicest cut of meat," Samuel was saying to the chef. Saul's mouth dropped open in bewilderment. And before he hardly had time to close it, the chef placed the choicest of meals before him. "Go ahead and eat," Samuel said. "I already told the chef how many I was inviting. This is for you. I've been expecting you."

Saul ate his meal in a daze. Why, God must have told this prophet that some VIP was coming and he had made a horrible mistake. No—no wait. Then how did he know about the donkeys? God must have told him about the donkeys. Who else?

Oh, well. The prophet had promised that in the morning he would clear everything up. He would tell Saul everything he wanted to know. There was nothing to do but wait. But

76

at the end of the feast, Saul didn't know any more than he knew before.

And When Will I Find Out?

Later that night, Saul lay on his mat staring into the moonlight. He was up on the roof of Samuel's house where he and his servant had gone to spend the night.[2] He and the prophet had talked far into the night about what was on the heart of every Israelite. You could hardly get into any conversation without talking about it. The signs of trouble were everywhere: it surrounded them. There were the ever-worrying Philistines on the west. And those rascals the Ammonites on the east. Israel wanted a king and everybody knew it.

But now Samuel had gone on downstairs to bed and Saul was alone.

It's Hard to Wait

The mysteries of the whole day and evening were whirling around in his head. The prophet had known him when he came in the city gates. He had been expecting him at the sacrificial feast. He had ordered the food for him. He had known about the donkeys. God had told him all these things.

Phew!

It was astonishing. But what and how did Saul fit in with all these things? Something was still missing in the puzzle. Would he ever find out what it was? It was hard to wait. He finally fell asleep, his head still whirling. The one question still danced in his head.

I Wish I Could Put It All Together

"Time to get up!"

It was Samuel's voice calling up to him. Saul sprang to

---

2. The roofs were flat and they were used for relaxation and for a garden. They could also pinch-hit for a guest room.

his feet. It was only daybreak. None of his questions were answered, he thought, as he washed and got ready for breakfast. How would this mysterious adventure end, he thought, as he started for the city gates with his servant. Samuel the prophet was walking along with them. It wasn't until he got to the city gates that he found out. "Send your servant on ahead," said Samuel. "I want to talk to you alone."

Saul motioned to his servant to go on. "I'll be with you in a minute," he said. His heart was pounding. He turned to look at Samuel.

Wow! This Is It?

"I have a special message for you," Samuel said quietly, "from the Lord."

This was it.

Saul watched with curiosity as Samuel took a flask of olive oil from his belt, and opened it. He stood in amazement as Samuel poured some of the oil on his head. He stood with unbelief as Samuel kissed him on the cheek. And then he nearly fell on his face. "I am doing this," Samuel said, "because the Lord has appointed you to be the king of Israel."

This was it?

It couldn't be! But Samuel was going on. "When you leave me," he said, "you will meet two men at Zelzah, in the land of Benjamin. They'll tell you that the donkeys have been found and that your father is worried about you. Now when you get to Tabor you'll meet three men coming toward you, who are on their way to worship God at the altar at Bethel."

Saul listened hard, trying to keep all this in his head.

"One will be carrying three goats," Samuel said, "one will have three loaves of bread, and the third will have a bottle of wine. They will greet you. And they'll offer you two of the loaves of bread. Take them."

"Yes, yes," said Saul. This was getting confusing.

"After that you will come to a place called God's hill."

"Yes, yes," Saul thought, trying to keep up.

"And as you arrive there, you will meet a band of prophets coming down the hill. They'll be playing a psaltery, a timbrel, a flute and a harp. And they'll be prophesying as they come. And at that time—"

There was *more?*

There was more.

"At that time, the Spirit of the Lord will come mightily upon you. And you will praise God with them in a way you've never done before."

This was too much.

"And what's more you will feel and act like a different person. And from that time on, the Lord will guide you."

Saul just stood and stared at Samuel. This was all too much. It was just overwhelming. He had a feeling that none of these things were really happening; he couldn't take it all in.

Is It for Real?

But as he turned away and started to leave Samuel, something happened.

His heart changed.

His mind changed.

He felt like a different person.

God had given him a completely new attitude.

He felt as if his feet had springs in them!

He caught up with his servant, his feet scarcely touching the ground. This was for real! This was for *real!*

Indeed It Is!

And on the journey home the evidence piled up. Everything Samuel had said came true—

The two men who told them their donkeys had been found.

The three men with the goats and bread and wine.

The band of prophets coming down the hill praising God.

It was indeed for real.

And as Saul found himself praising God with them, he knew it for sure. It was indeed for real.

It's Nice to Know When to Keep Your Mouth Shut

"Where in the world did you go?" said his uncle, when he got back home.

Saul thought back over all that had happened. "We went to look for the donkeys," he said, "but we couldn't find them. So we went to the prophet Samuel and asked him where they were."

"Oh? And what did he say?" said his uncle.

"Oh, he said the donkeys had been found," said Saul. Should he go on? After all, there was plenty to brag about. He'd been anointed king. Should he talk about it? Did Samuel tell him he could? He thought back over it. No. Samuel did *not* tell him he could.

"And?" said his uncle.

"He just said the donkeys had been found," Saul said.

He had just displayed his first act of wisdom.

It's a Good Idea to Be Modest, Too

It was a great day at Mizpah. There was a huge convocation[3] from all over Israel gathered there. Samuel had called them together. There was something important afoot. Was this the day he would give them the king he had promised? And whoever would he be? The air was crackling with excitement.

When Samuel raised his hands for silence, everyone listened intently. You never saw a quieter audience. Not a man as much as shuffled his feet. Samuel gave them the message. And it was straight from God.

"I brought you out of Egypt. I rescued you from your enemies. But although I've done so much for you, you've rejected Me. You said, 'We want a king instead!' So you want a king instead? All right! Present yourselves before Me by tribes and clans."

That was it.

3. Thousands of people—sort of like a super-rally.

There was a great silence. Something tremendously important was going to happen.

Samuel called the tribal leaders together. The whole assembly waited for the announcement.

"The king will be from the tribe of Benjamin!"

Every man in the tribe of Benjamin quivered from stem to stern.

Now each family in the tribe of Benjamin was told to march by.

"The family of Matrites is chosen!" the announcement came.

Everyone waited, hardly daring to breathe.

Now this was it. Who was the king? Who was he?

"Saul, the son of Kish!"

Saul, the son of Kish?!?

Those who didn't know him, said "Who is *he?*"

And those who did know him said, "Who—*him?!?*"

And there was all hubbub and confusion and they all tried to find Saul, the son of Kish.

More important than *who* was he, was—*where* was he?

Nobody could find him!

He had absolutely disappeared.

But How Modest Can You Get?

It's nice to be modest,[4] but this could be the most ridiculous case of modesty on record. Saul was found hiding—you'll never guess it—Saul was found hiding among the baggage that the people in the traveling assembly had brought with them!

They found him and hauled him out. And led him to the high spot where Samuel was, for everybody to see. Saul's big moment had come. And all he wanted to do was run and hide. Nothing cocky about him, no indeed.

But when the people saw him!

Wow!

4. Not "stuck-up."

How tall! How majestic looking! He even *looked* like a king!

"Long live the king!" they shouted. And the noise echoed through the hills and valleys like thunder. "Long live the kinnnnnnnnnng!"

It Was a Package Deal

So the kingship was given to Saul. He was not only declared king, but the honor was given to him in a package. There were goodies that came with it.

Samuel drew up all the rights and duties of a king, so Saul had a constitution. And the Bible tells us that a band of men whose hearts God had touched, promised to support him and become his constant companions—so he had a cabinet. And so with a constitution and a cabinet and a prophet like Samuel—he had the works! He couldn't miss.

How Could You Fail?

Talk about getting off to a good start! His father had a beautiful home. And he had the support of the people of Israel. And if anybody wanted to pick an argument, he was head and shoulders taller than anybody else. And such fine qualities of character! He was wise, he was modest—he was everything. He could have easily been voted the man most likely to succeed. With all these advantages and all these gifts and all these favors—it would be pretty hard to fail.

What About You?

Are you off to a good start? Everything going your way?

Well, all things being equal, the chances are you can finish what you start, and in fine shape, too. But not without God.

"God who began the good work within you will keep right on helping you . . . until his task within you is finally finished . . ." (Phil. 1:6, *TLB*).

Read it again. *Who* is able to finish?

Don't forget it.

HAVE YOU FORGOTTEN SOMETHING?

1 Samuel 11

"Testing—Testing—1-2-3"

It's the first thing you do with a public address system or a tape recorder or a microphone. You want to see if it works. It's absolutely no good if it's just there to look at. It has to work.

Naturally the first thing the Israelites wanted to know was whether this new king-business was working.

They didn't have to wait long to find out. For it wasn't long before there was trouble afoot. The Ammonites began to get nippy.

Testing—Testing—Help!

What? Weren't the Philistines enough? Did the Ammonites have to get in on the act, too? Well, actually the Ammonites had to get in on the act *again*. Those pesky rascals had been enemies of the Israelites for a long, long time.[1] And now they were at it again. And what did they attack? Why, poor little Jabesh-gilead, 'way across the Jordan—so far from the stronger cities of Israel that the people didn't have a chance. Who would come to their aid?

Nobody.

A treaty! That was the only answer, they thought. We'll make a deal with the enemy. Offer to be their slaves before they kill us all.

They sent messengers to the Ammonite king. Fellow by the name of Nahash.

"A deal!" they cried. "A deal!"

"Good," said Nahash, "I'll make a deal with you. On one condition."

"Yes, yes!" thought the Israelites. Any condition. If it isn't too unreasonable.

Unreasonable? It was impossible!

The deal was, that he would gouge out the right eye of every one of them!

In those days it was the custom for the warriors to hold their shields before their faces during battle. Which eye did they cover? The left eye. And which eye did they use to peek over the shield so they could see to fight? You guessed it. The right eye. It was one of the cruelest "deals" on record. It was the kind of a deal you didn't rush into.

"Wait!" the leaders of Jabesh-gilead cried. "Give us seven days. Just hold off for seven days. That's all we ask."

And they sent a messenger off with a frantic SOS.

To where? Why, to Saul's hometown of course. Where else would they turn but to their king?

Let's see if this king-business was working.

It SEEMS to Be Working

And where was the king? Why he was out plowing in the

---

1. They were the descendants of Lot. Remember him?

field! This king-business hadn't really got going yet, you see. There was no palace. There was no big capital city for the government. Having a king was all very new to Israel. It was all very new to Saul, too. He hadn't got going yet because he hadn't had a problem.

When he got back to town from the fields, he knew he had one, all right. Everybody in the town was crying.

"What's the matter?" he said. "Why is everyone crying?" And they told him the dreadful news. And you never saw a new king get going so fast in your life. He cut up his two oxen in little pieces. And he sent the pieces with messengers all over the country of Israel. "If you don't rally around and come at once to defend your brothers, this should happen to *your* oxen! Watch it!"

Then you never saw an army get mobilized so fast in your life. They came swarming in from every direction, thousands of them. Saul sent the messengers from Jabesh-gilead back to their frightened city. "You'll be rescued tomorrow before noon," he said, "and I've got 330,000 men here to prove it. Hold fast till we get there."

It would be hard to imagine the joy in that city when the message arrived. This king-business was working!

This King Is Full of Smarts

Now you never saw strategy planned so fast in your life. They had to hurry! There was not a moment to lose. Their seven days were almost up. The messengers flew back and forth between Saul and Saul's army and the fighting men in Jabesh. They had bulletins, late bulletins and late-late bulletins. And this is what they did.

It's Working, It's Working!

The men of Jabesh sent messengers out to their enemies. "We surrender!" they said. "We'll come out to you, and you can do with us as you wish. We accept your deal."

87

Tomorrow.

That "tomorrow" was very important. They needed the night to complete their plans.

The hours ticked away.

Nahash waited.

The people in Jabesh waited.

Saul was marching his army across the plains through the darkness toward Jabesh. As they drew close to Jabesh, they marched almost soundlessly; they hardly dared step on a twig. Now the orders were given in whispers. Saul divided his army into three sections. It was all planned. They marched toward Nahash's army—one section to the left, one section to the right, one section head-on. The Ammonites slept on, their weapons lying on the ground by their sides. They didn't know it, but they were surrounded.

The first streaks of dawn crept across the sky. The first birds began to stir. And then—

"Attack! To your arms! Fight! Rescue your brothers! To the battle! Fight as you've never fought before!"

The Ammonites thought the sky had fallen in!

The rest was bedlam! The Israelites scattered the Ammonites like buckshot, in all directions. By noon, what was left of their army was so badly scattered, there weren't two of them left together. Every man was running wildly—and alone—for his own life; there wasn't even a "buddy" system.

We Have a King—Who Needs Anything More?

After the dust had settled, Samuel spoke to them. And he put it in a nutshell, all of it. He just tied up all the loose ends. If there was any doubt in anybody's mind, he cinched it. "Come on," he said, "let's all go to Gilgal and reconfirm[2] Saul as our king."

Saul was the hero of the day, no doubt about it.

2. Promise it over again.

Have You Forgotten Something?

Once they were gathered at Gilgal, they crowned Saul king. And Samuel made the coronation speech. It was a combination thanksgiving, pep-talk and memory-lesson all rolled into one. And he pulled no punches. "All right!" he cried. "Here's the king you've chosen. Look him over. You asked for him. And the Lord has answered your request."

"Hoooray!" they cried back.

"But don't forget," Samuel went on. They were silent, listening. "Don't forget the Lord. Now if you will fear and worship the Lord and listen to His commandments and not rebel against Him—*if both you and your king follow the Lord your God*—then all will be well."

You could have heard a twig drop.

"BUT!"

They jumped.

"If you rebel against the Lord and refuse to listen to Him—watch it!"

They shuffled their feet and listened on.

"Worship the Lord with true enthusiasm," Samuel shouted, "and don't turn your back on Him in any way. And always remember—other gods can't help you!"

No indeed, they knew that. But wouldn't having a prophet like Samuel help them? And a king like Saul? Samuel went on as if he could read their thoughts. "As for me," he cried, "I will continue to teach you those things that are good and right. I will continue to pray for you. BUT—"

A shiver ran through the whole multitude.

"BUT!" he shouted, "there is one thing you must not forget. Trust the LORD and sincerely worship HIM. Think of all the tremendous things He has done for you!"

Ah, yes. Have you forgotten something? Don't forget God. Make a note.

"But," he went on, "if you continue to sin—"

Then he dropped the thunderbolt.

"You *and* your king—will be destroyed."

89

Better Not!

Yes—"having a king" was working. It was working very well. There was just one thing never to forget.

You'd better not forget God.

What About You?

Sometimes on the doors of hotels there's a sign saying: HAVE YOU FORGOTTEN SOMETHING? That's so you can go back and check to make sure you haven't.

Might be a good idea to tack a sign like that on the back of your bedroom door. And add to it the verses:

"Trust the Lord and sincerely worship him" (1 Sam. 12:24, *TLB*).

"In all thy ways acknowledge him, and he shall direct thy paths" (Prov. 3:6, *KJV*).

No matter who your leader is—don't forget God.

YOU CAN'T GET THERE FROM HERE— WITHOUT GOD

1 Samuel 14

"Let's go over to the Philistines," the young Israelite man said to his companion. "Are you willing to go with me? Just the two of us?"

Over? *Over?*

Why there was no way to go but *down.*

They were standing on the edge of a cliff.

And the Philistines were on top of another cliff across the way!

It was like standing on the edge of a mini Grand Canyon and saying, "Let's go over to the other side." The young man's companion could have said, "You just can't get there from here." It was a rough scramble down. And a dangerous trek across the pass. Then an even rougher climb up the other side. And up to what? To fight a whole garrison of Philistines? Just the *two* of them?

93

They stared for a while, across to the other side. And then, "Fine," the companion said. "Do as you think best. And whatever you decide to do—I'm with you—all the way."

"All right, then. This is what we'll do . . ."

The Philistines we know. And the Israelites we know. But who were these two young men? And were they out of their minds?

Well, it all began this way . . .

This Is How It Was

Saul had been ruling for some time now, and doing a very good job of it, too. He had sent most of his army back to their homes. But he kept a standing army of three thousand on duty at all times.

The Israelites' enemies were forever yapping at their heels like a pack of pesky dogs. If it wasn't the Ammonites, it was the Philistines.

This time it was the Philistines.

Now it was pretty hard to argue with the Philistines, for they were doing more than yapping at Israel's borders. They had made inroads and were occupying the country. They were very very cruel. And very, very clever. And besides, they had discovered the secret of smelting iron so they had all the iron weapons—which were far superior to the bronze weapons of the Israelites. An Israelite didn't have a chance to get hold of an iron weapon. He could buy iron *farm tools* from the Philistines. But an iron *weapon* was a no-no.

The Philistines had a neat way of handling this. They just didn't allow their blacksmiths in the land of Israel. Whenever the Israelites needed to sharpen their farm tools or get them fixed, they had to take them to a Philistine blacksmith. And they had to pay through the nose, at fancy prices. Out of sight!

The only way the Israelites could sneak in any iron weapons was to make them out of farm tools.

And This Is How the Action Started

Anyhow, Saul divided his army of three thousand men into three battalions, a thousand men in each. He took command of the two battalions and camped in the hill country between Bethel and Michmash. The other battalion was under the command of Saul's son, Jonathan. He was stationed at Gibeah. Now the Philistines were stationed at Geba about three miles north of Gibeah. If this sounds confusing it's because it *is* confusing and you have to have a map to figure it out.

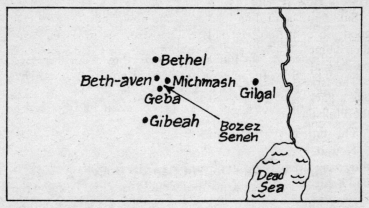

But it wasn't confusing to either the Israelites or Philistines because they knew the country. When we say Paul Revere rode from Charleston to Lexington, or that the Pilgrims landed at Plymouth Rock at Plymouth, Massachusetts, it's easy for us to understand because it's our own country. When you run into names like Gibeah and Michmash, the going gets rough. Don't be afraid of odd names. They're only towns and places, just like in our own country.

ANYHOW . . .

A strange series of events began to take place. It was like a gigantic game, each player making his move, then watching to see what move the other player would make.

It began with Saul's son, Jonathan. Under Saul's orders,

he attacked the Philistine garrison at Geba and wiped it out. And moved *his* troops in. He had struck the first blow in the war of independence. He had made the first move. Now the players were off and away, and nobody could stop them.

The news spread like wildfire throughout all the camps of the Philistines. And Saul "blew his horn"—he sent heralds throughout all the cities of Israel to announce the news. "And what do the Philistines think of us now?" the message said. "We have made ourselves odious with the Philistines. To put it bluntly, they think we stink!" The idea was that every fighting man in Israel was to come arunning to help. And come running they did. From every direction. And Saul mobilized them there at Gilgal.

And what of the Philistines? Well, they were impressed, to put it mildly. In fact they were downright frightened. These Israelites were good. They were *too* good.

It was the Philistines' move now. And it had better be a good one.

It was.

"Anything You Can Do, We Can Do Better"

They amassed[1] an army that would scare any Israelite right out of his toga.[2] Horsemen—thousands of them. Chariots—thousands of them. And foot soldiers—there were so many of them they were like the sand on the seashore. There seemed to be no end to them. And they advanced and pitched camp in Michmash. And waited.

Now the next move was up to the Israelites.

"I'm Not Scared, I'm Just Cautious"

Well, the men of Israel moved all right. They began to move in all directions.

The *wrong* directions.

1. Scraped together.
2. That's a robe.

96

Some of them hid in caves and holes in the rocks. Some of them hid in thickets. Some of them even hid in tombs and cisterns.[3] And some of them crossed the Jordan River and escaped to the land of Gad and Gilead. It was the biggest *dis*organized move in all directions in the history of battles. A scareder bunch of soldiers you never saw in all your life.

Every time Saul looked around, a few more of his men were gone. He hung in there though, and the men who stayed and hung in there with him were trembling in their sandals, at what was to happen to them.

Hurry Up and Wait

And what was Saul's next move? It was a hard one to make. Or rather, *not* to make. For Saul's next move was to *wait*.

What?

Yes. Samuel had told him earlier that he would be there in seven days. For what? Why, to offer a burnt offering and a peace offering to the Lord. And Saul was to *wait for his arrival*. Now you know and I know that this is one of the hardest things to do when you want ACTION. Wait? When the sky will fall in if you don't do something? Wait? When your problem is going to do you in if you don't solve it? Wait? When everything in you is screaming "Do something!"? Why, sometimes the hardest thing in the world to do, is wait.

Saul's men were slipping away from him by the dozens— then by the hundreds. The hardest "move" he had to make was to wait.

"I'd Rather Do It Myself"

Saul waited. One day. More men slipped away. Two days. More men gone.

Three days. Those crazy Philistines would attack any minute. Four days. *More* men gone. Should he wait any longer?

---

3. A place for storing water.

Five days. Six. Maybe Samuel would come a day early. The day went by. More of Saul's men slipped away. The night of the sixth day. Samuel would come tomorrow. He *had* to come tomorrow. Seven days. Scarcely ten miles away were the Philistines, ready to pour down and crush him. Samuel, come *on*—what are you waiting for? The seventh day. And no Samuel. The problem was getting bigger and there was nobody here to solve it. Have you forgotten us entirely? The seventh day slipped away. And so did more soldiers. Still no Samuel.

Well, it was no use. Samuel wasn't going to show up. If the thing was going to get done, Saul would have to do it himself, he decided. "Bring me a burnt offering and a peace offering," he said to his aides. "I'm going to make the offerings to the Lord myself."

Well, they did. And he did. It was a good idea, yes? It was a good idea, *no*.

And it was no sooner finished, than who should turn up but—you guessed it.

Samuel.

"What have you done?" Samuel said.

"Well," Saul stuttered, "when I saw my men were scattering from me in all directions—"

"You have done a foolish thing," the prophet shook his head.

"But you hadn't arrived by the time you said you would."

"Foolish, foolish."

"But the Philistines are at Michmash. They're ready for battle."

"You shouldn't have done it."

"So I said to myself, I said the Philistines are ready to march against us and—"

"Ah. You should have waited."

"Well—I didn't really want to do it. But finally I just did. My conscience told me I shouldn't."

"Mmmmmm."

"It was a difficult decision. I really had to force myself to do this."

The Next Move Was All Gloom

The days that followed were black ones. Samuel had left. He had gone back to Gibeah in the land of Benjamin. Saul was left to brood over the mistake he had made in not waiting for Samuel—and God—to act. He hadn't shown much faith—but what was a man to do, with a problem like that hanging over his head, he argued to himself.

Augggh.

The next move was filled with gloom. Saul and his son, Jonathan, and the six hundred men who were left, set up their camp in Geba in the land of Benjamin. The Philistines were still at Michmash. And they were sending out raiders in all directions. Things were going uncomfortably from bad to worse. There was no sense hoping now. Nothing was going to turn out all right.

—Or Would Have Been—

It was at this gloomy point that it happened.[4]

The two young men stood on the edge of the cliff and said, "Let's go over to the Philistine garrison." Yes, you guessed it. One of the young men was Jonathan. And the other young man was his armor-bearer.[5]

"Let's go over to the garrison of the Philistines," Jonathan said. "Perhaps the Lord will do a miracle for us."

"A miracle?"

"Of course, a miracle. For it makes no difference to the Lord how many enemy troops there are. Or how many of *us* there are either."

"I'm with you. All the way."

4. The "you can't get there from here" business.
5. An armor-bearer was a bodyguard to his master. He also carried the weapons—sort of like a caddy. He did some fighting too. It was a rough job and called for a brave man.

"All right, then," said Jonathan. "This is what we'll do."

"We'll climb down this side and keep under the crag.[6] And then we'll go across. They won't see us until we get by the crag on their side."

"Then what?"

"Then, when they see us—if they shout at us, 'Stay where you are or we'll kill you'—we'll stop. And wait. BUT. If they say, 'Come on up and fight!' Then we'll do just that. It'll be God's signal and He'll help us defeat them. Got it?"

"Got it."

So they let themselves over the edge. And began to work their way down over the jagged rocks. They kept under the great crag called Seneh. Then they crossed. Then under the crag on the north called Bozez. And then—

Suddenly they were in plain sight. The Philistines saw them coming.

"Look!" they shouted. "The Israelites are coming! They're crawling out of their holes!"

Jonathan and his armor-bearer stood still, looking up, shading their eyes and squinting. They waited.

"Come on up here and we'll show you how to fight!"

That was it. That was *it*. That was the signal. "Come on!" Jonathan said. "Climb up right behind me. For the Lord will help us wipe them out!" And they clambered up on their hands and knees.

"At 'em!"

They clung to the rocks, slipping, hanging on, clambering up again.

They got closer. And closer. And closer. Almost to the top. And then—

—But God Was There!

"Over the top!"

---

6. A big jagged rock sticking out from the cliff. There were two of them, one on each side.

They scrambled over the top, first Jonathan, then his armor-bearer close behind. "Plow into them!" cried Jonathan. "Plow into them! Give me my sword!" And the two of them charged into the Philistines for all the world, as if they were a great army instead of just two young men. They swung their weapons left and right. Jonathan knocked them down and his armor-bearer came close behind and finished the job. Within minutes, twenty Philistines had been killed. And then—

Everything seemed to happen at once. The rest of the Philistines panicked and drew back, dropping their weapons behind them.

And then the very earth began to tremble. And—

EARTHQUAKE! EARTHQUAAAAAAAKE!!!!!

The Philistines dropped their weapons and staggered. The very earth seemed to give way beneath them and they staggered and fell as they tried to run. And there was as much terror and confusion on that battlefield as if Jonathan and his armor-bearer had been an army of thousands. God was with them!

On the other side, the lookouts in Saul's army jumped to attention, their eyes boggling.

What was this?

The vast army of the Philistines was melting away in all directions! The ground was trembling on the other cliff! The soldiers were staggering, falling, running in confusion! And noise! You couldn't hear yourself for the din!

"Find out who isn't here!" Saul ordered. "Who's missing?"

And some soldiers ran to check. They came back, breathless and amazed. "It's Jonathan! Jonathan is gone! And his bodyguard too! We can't find them anywhere!"

Then they all had the same thought at once.

They looked across the cliff to the other cliff. "Look at them!" And they stood staring in amazement.

Those crazy Philistines were going around in circles—hither and thither and to and fro—without any idea of where they were going. They acted as if they had gone berserk!

"They're killing each other!"

"Good grief!"

"They are! They're killing each other!"

"They're so mixed up they don't know who the enemy is!"

Well this was no time to stop and think. This was the time for immediate action. "What are we waiting for?" they thought. And the cry went out—

"CHARGE!"

And Saul's army scrambled over the edge of the cliff, under the crags, up the other side, on their hands and knees.

First there were a few of them.

And then there were more of them.

And then there were dozens of them.

And then there were HUNDREDS of them. For the ones who had hidden themselves came out of hiding. Out from everywhere. Out from the caves and the holes in the rocks. Out from the thickets. Out from the tombs and cisterns. Out they came, scrambling up the side of the cliff to the Philistines. On and on they went, the Philistines running and falling, the Israelites chasing them as far as Beth-aven!

What a day! When God fought for Israel!

The Philistines ran like mad toward their own land.

Saul and his army, with the help of God, finished the job. But it was started by two young men who plowed into the enemy all by themselves, and dared to believe that God would help them.

It was a story that seemed to have a perfect ending. Except for one thing.

Aw—You've Gone and Spoiled It

That business about Saul.

He had not been willing to wait for God. It seemed like such a little thing. Little but pesky.

Pesky?

Yes, pesky. Because little things have a habit of growing

into bigger things. And Saul had never been sorry for what he had done. And he had never asked God to forgive him.

Bad business, that.

What a shame.

What About You?

The chances are, you aren't standing on the edge of a cliff thinking about licking a whole army on the top of another cliff. But that doesn't mean you don't have any problems.

Do you have a problem that seems so big that "you just can't get there from here"? Have you talked to God about it?

He's just as able to solve a big problem as a little one, you know. Jonathan put it all in a nutshell: "For it makes no difference to him (God) how many enemy troops there are!" (1 Sam. 14:6, *TLB*).

And watch out for the *little* things. Snitching on the rules in *little* ways. It's the little things that can trip you up, you know.

Why?

Because they multiply. And they have a habit of getting bigger. Disobeying in *little* ways can get to be a habit that will do you in.

THE RULE-BENDER
1 Samuel 15:1-35

A rule-bender is a person who obeys some[1] of the rules all of the time and all of the rules *some* of the time.[2] But he seldom obeys *all* of the rules *all* of the time. And he seldom obeys the rules as they *are*. He obeys them only after he has bent them a bit, to his liking.

Bending rules can be developed into a fine art if you practice it. And if you keep at it long enough, it becomes a lifetime habit. And you find yourself bending rules without even thinking about it.

One strange thing about rule-bending is that the bent rule never gets hurt. It is always the *bender* who gets hurt. And if the bender happens to be a leader, then of course the matter is a lot more complicated. For the people following him sometimes get hurt too.

1. A few.
2. If it's convenient.

Profile of a Rule Bender

We read a great deal about "profiles" these days. We have a "profile" of a skyjacker, a "profile" of a criminal, a "profile" of an astronaut—

It's sort of a "picture" of what the person is apt to be like. It's a rundown on the pattern of his behavior. And it goes something like this:

"But I Don't *Break* Rules"

"No, sir. When I play the game I play it fair and square. And when I'm told to do something, I do it. I was told to clean my room and I did it all right. In record time, too. I even finished ahead of schedule."

Did you now? And could you guarantee that the job would bear inspection?[3]

Well, one look at Saul's life[4] and it was apparent that he was no rule *breaker* either. He did his jobs right on schedule and he did them very well, too. And now that he was "securely in the saddle" as a successful king, he sent his armies out in every direction against Israel's enemies. All of them.

Moab.

Ammon.

Edom.

The kings of Zobah.

And the Philistines. Always the Philistines.

The Bible tells us that Israel fought with the Philistines all through Saul's lifetime. Yes, Saul was the conquering hero. And when he was told to do something, he did it. In record time, and right on schedule. And when Samuel told him that God wanted him to settle accounts with the Amalekites—

The *Amalekites!* Where'd *they* come from?

Oh, they'd been there all the time. Right from the start. They had attacked the Israelites right after they got out of

3. Would you be willing to have somebody check it out?
4. If you didn't look too closely.

Egypt and were on their way to the Promised Land. Joshua had engaged them in successful battle.[5] And a year later when the Israelites had attempted to enter the Promised Land, the Amalekites had driven back.[6] And during the years when the Israelites were trying to settle their land, the Amalekites were yapping at their heels.

But now the Lord had decided it was time to settle accounts and put an end to the whole pesky business.

ANYHOW—

Samuel told Saul to destroy the Amalekites. *All* of them who fell into his hands. And to destroy everything they owned. *Everything*.

Well, Saul did it, all right. Just as he was told. He took 210,000 soldiers and swept across the Sinai Peninsula and the Arabian Desert. And before he got through with the Amalekites, they were destroyed—from the wilderness of Shur[7] to Havilah.[8] Which is like saying from Philadelphia to Washington.

But would the job bear inspection? Would Saul be willing to have someone check it out?

"I Just Bend Them a Little"

"Of course I didn't do it *exactly* as I was told."

No, you sure didn't. What about those things your mother didn't want you to have and asked you to get rid of? Yes, and while we're at it, what about that stuff you shoved under the bed so you wouldn't have to put it away? And those things you were supposed to sort out and put in their proper places? They're stashed in a heap in the back of your closet, aren't they?

Aren't they?

And your homework assignment is there too.

5. He clobbered them.
6. Read Numbers 14:43,45.
7. The area east of the Suez Canal.
8. Near the southern point of the Red Sea.

No, you sure *didn't* do it exactly as you were told.

Well, Saul didn't do *exactly* as he was told either. He captured the king of the Amalekites. Fellow by the name of Agag. But he saved him alive, instead of killing him as he had been ordered to. And he could not resist the temptation to make a profit out of the deal. He ordered his men to keep the best of the sheep and the best of the young oxen and the best of the lambs. They kept everything that would make a profit. Only the animals that were old or feeble or sick or crippled were destroyed.

Saul did what he'd been told to do. But not *exactly*. He hadn't *broken* the rules. He had just *bent* them a little.

"Then I Go Off All Pleased with Myself"

"Of course I fudged a little. But no harm done. As long as nobody got hurt. And nobody found out. What's the difference?"

This is exactly what Saul did. And this was apparently the way Saul *felt*. Pleased with himself. He stopped at Carmel on the way home and put up a monument[9] to celebrate his victory. And then he went on to Gilgal.

It was there that Samuel caught up with him.

When Samuel finally found him, Saul was all wide-eyed innocence. "Greetings!" he said. "I did exactly as I was told to do. The job is done." And in spite of all the cattle and all the loot around him, he actually believed he was getting away with it!

"Whoops—I'm Caught"

"So I'm caught. They found the stuff under the bed. And the stuff stashed away in my closet. And my homework assignment. Ugh. I guess the jig is up. I'm caught dead-to-rights."

---

9. A sort of trophy of his victory.

And so it was with Saul. "I've carried out the Lord's command," he told Samuel.

Samuel gave him a long hard look. "What was all the bleating of sheep and lowing of oxen I heard?" he demanded.

Saul was caught red-handed and dead-to-rights. The jig was up.

What do you do when the jig is up?

"I'll Think of a Way Out"

"I'm quick. And I'm slippery. And clever too. And when I'm caught, I can think of something faster than you can say, 'What have you done?' I might have to admit that I did it. But I can always think of a good reason *why.*"

Well, Saul was quick and slippery and clever too. The jig was up. Samuel had seen the loot. Well, all right, Samuel had *heard* the loot. Saul had to think fast.

"Well, it's true that I didn't do *exactly* as I was told. My armies spared the best of the sheep and the oxen," he said. "But—but—"

Why, why? Hurry up and think of a reason *why.*

"But the people wanted them for sacrifices to the Lord your God," he whined. "And we have destroyed everything else. Why, we destroyed all the feeble cattle—and all the sick—"

"Stop!" Samuel shouted.

Saul stopped.

"Listen to what the Lord told me last night," said Samuel.

Saul listened.

And Samuel pulled no punches.

"My Excuse Isn't Working?"

"A while ago, when you were modest and didn't think you were a big-shot," Samuel said, "God made you king of Israel."

"Yes," said Saul.

"And now He gave you this job to do."

"Yes, yes."

"He told you to destroy the Amalekites."

"Yes."

"*All* of them. And their things. *Everything.*"

"Yes."

"And not keep anything to make a profit."

"Right." Saul's voice was getting weaker. He was in for it, and he knew it.

"Then," thundered Samuel, "WHY DIDN'T YOU OBEY HIM??? WHY DID YOU DO THE VERY THING GOD TOLD YOU NOT TO DO?"

Phew.

"I'll Stick to My Guns"

"This is no time to back down. If I back down, all is lost. I *never* back down. I just keep on insisting. If they keep accusing me, I just insist harder. If they keep on—I act hurt. If they get tough about it, I talk faster and louder. Sometimes you can bluff it out that way."

Well, Saul tried that one too. "But I *have* obeyed the Lord," he insisted. "I've done what He told me to do. I killed the Amalekites, just as He said. Of course I did save King Agag."

It wasn't working. Samuel just shook his head sadly. "Before I even came here," he said, "the Lord told me, 'I'm sorry that I ever made Saul king. For he has refused to obey Me again.'"

No, it *wasn't* working. Have to talk faster.

"They Made Me Do It"

"It isn't working? Then I make a quick switch. I blame somebody else. And the more I practice the better I get at it. And the quicker I can think of somebody else to blame. With enough practice, I can think of somebody to blame the minute I see that it isn't working."

Saul tried that one too. "And—and it was only when my troops *demanded* it," he sputtered, "that I let them keep the

110

best of the sheep and the oxen—and the loot. Eh—to sacrifice to the Lord, of course."

Phew. That was a close one.

"Nothing's Going to Work"

"The jig's up. None of my tricks work. Nothing I say does any good. I'm caught dead-to-rights. I'm backed in a corner. I guess I'll have to admit it."

Well, Saul was in a corner too, but good. There was no escape. All his talk about sacrificing the animals to the Lord wasn't going over very well. Samuel was looking at him sadly. "Do you think the Lord takes more pleasure in your sacrifices than He does in your obedience?" he said. "You say you saved these animals to sacrifice to Him? He's much more interested in your *listening* to Him."

No, it wasn't going over very well at all.

"Obedience is far better than sacrifice," Samuel went on. "Why, Saul, your stubbornness is as bad as worshiping idols. You've rejected God!"

This was serious. Samuel meant business.

"—And because you've rejected the Word of God—*He has rejected you!*"

What?

"Yes! He has rejected you as king!"

What? This was catastrophic![10]

There was only one more way to go. And that was—admit it.

"I Did It, I Did It—BUT—"

"I admit I did it. But I have a good reason. I was afraid everybody'd be angry with me if I didn't."

There. *That* ought to do it.

Admit it, yes. But you can leave yourself a loophole.

That was the way Saul decided to go. "I've sinned," he

10. This was a knockout blow!

111

finally admitted. "And I disobeyed the command of the Lord—BUT—"

Oh, oh. Here it comes.

"I did it because I was afraid of the people. I just did what they demanded. I was afraid not to."

Saul? Afraid of the people? What a pity. What kind of a king was this? If he was telling the truth, was it more important to be worried about what people thought, than it was to be worried about obeying God?

And was he more concerned with his popularity than he was about pleasing God?

Was he afraid of the people or was he still bluffing?

"Let's Forget It"

"I never say I'm sorry. Tell you what. Let's forget it ever happened. Let me off the hook. Let's go on like before. Just as if everything were all right."

Go on the way it was before? As if everything were all right? And you don't intend to change? You *are* asking for trouble!

Did Saul mean to go this far? Yes, indeed, Saul meant to go this far. "Please pardon my sin!" he cried. "Go with me now to worship the Lord."

It didn't work. "It's no use," Samuel said, "you've rejected the commandment of God. Now He has rejected you—as king."

It wasn't working, it wasn't working. And that was all Saul was worried about.

He never did say he was sorry.

"Pretend It Isn't So"

Pretend it isn't so? And maybe it'll go away? You just want to go on fooling people? As long as nobody else knows about it you can pretend it isn't so, eh? And after a while you believe it yourself.

How foolish.

You're on the wrong track. On the road that's going no-where. You can't win.

Saul tried to the very last to pretend it wasn't so.

Samuel turned to go. "Wait!" Saul cried, and he grabbed at Samuel and tried to hold him back—

And tore his robe!

Samuel turned and looked Saul square in the eye. "See?" he said. "The Lord has torn your kingdom from you today, just as you've torn my robe. And He's going to give it to somebody else."

And still Saul did not say he was sorry. All he could think of was saving his face before the people. "All *right!*" he said, "I've sinned. But don't make me look foolish before my people. I don't want a public scandal. You can at least honor me before the leaders and before my people by going with me to worship the Lord your God. Oh, *please* don't make me look foolish!"

But he *still* did not say he was sorry.

You Forgot Something

With all your huffing and puffing, you forgot one thing. The most important thing of all. You're not sorry. You don't intend to change.

Some rule-benders are determined to *remain* rule-benders all their lives. What a pity.

Well, Samuel finally agreed and went with Saul to worship the Lord.

Then he turned sadly away and went home to Ramah. And Saul returned to Gibeah. Without ever saying he was sorry.

You Blew It

If you've gone through all these stages. And you're not sorry. And you don't intend to change—

You blew it.

Yes, rule-bending can be very risky business. And the greatest danger lies in not being sorry.

The old rule-bender, Saul, went back to being king. But the tragedy is that he didn't intend to change. He intended to go on bending rules.

Yes, one strange thing about rule-bending is that the bent rule never gets hurt. It's always the *bender* who gets hurt. In this case, it was Saul.[11]

One of the saddest verses in the Bible is: "Samuel never saw Saul again, but he mourned constantly for him, and the Lord was sorry that he had ever made Saul king of Israel."[12]

What About You?

Are you a rule-bender?

The trouble with bending the rules is, you can think of so many excuses when you're caught. After all, you didn't break the rule—you just *bent* it.

So stop your huffing and puffing. Or you'll huff and you'll puff and you'll blow your testimony in. You either did it or you didn't. Which is it? Level with those in authority over you. Level with yourself. And level with God.

"Has the Lord as much pleasure in your burnt offerings and sacrifices as in your obedience? Obedience is far better than sacrifice. He is much more interested in your listening to him than in your offering the fat of rams to him" (1 Sam. 15:22, *TLB*).

11. More about him later.
12. 1 Samuel 15:35, *TLB*.

GUESS WHO'S GOING TO BE A—WHAT?

1 Samuel 16

Samuel We Know—

Samuel was in his home town of Ramah, grieving. He'd been grieving ever since that dark day when he had told King Saul that God had rejected him. He'd left the king then—never to go back. But he hadn't forgotten.

Samuel still went from town to town, holding religious services and offering sacrifices. Yes, he was still a circuit preacher.[1] But always, underneath everything he did, was his great sorrow over Saul. Saul, who'd shown such promise, who'd had such a wonderful beginning—and now there was no place for him to go but down . . .

And Saul We Know—

King Saul was in his fortress palace. He was a far cry from the tall handsome man Samuel had anointed king many years

1. Traveling preacher. Remember?

before. Then he had been very modest—now he was very arrogant.[2] Then he was full of get-up-and-go—now he was full of sit-down-and-mope.

He was skidding down hill, and the ride was a fast one. He had disobeyed God again and again. And the saddest part of all was that he'd never been sorry—he had never asked God to forgive him. And so God had left him. And now he was torn apart by the spirit of anger and suspicion and cruelty—and jealousy.

When he was in one of his good moods, he strutted back and forth in the palace, as if he owned the world. But when he was in a bad mood, he would sit and stare into space for hours, and even his officers and closest aides hardly dared speak to him.

Sometimes he would fly into a fury, and everyone would scurry for cover to get out of his way. He would bellow until the flames in the lamps scudded backward, as if they too were trying to get out of his way. He was on the skids and he knew it. And he was still blaming everybody else. The habit was strong. He'd had it for years. Everybody was "out to get him." Everybody was "going to fail him." It never crossed his mind once that he had failed God.

The misery and gloom in the palace spilled over the whole country. Everyone felt it. It seemed to be in the very air—*"Well, we're certainly in a mess—what's going to happen now?"*

Indeed there was nowhere to go but down. Everything looked hopeless.

But Who's THIS??

The young man scampered up on a crag[3] and called his sheep to follow him. He called them with a deep throaty sound, and they scampered up behind him, as he called each

2. Stuck up.
3. A big jagged rock.

one by name. He reached down with his staff and helped the weak ones up. And he shaded his eyes and looked out over the level place beyond. There was fresh pasture just up ahead. He waited until the last straggler had scrambled up and was safe. Then he got ahead of his little flock and led them with long, sure strides toward the pasture land. They all followed, bleating and stumbling over each other.

He was a good-looking lad, tall and strong with reddish hair—and beautiful eyes. He called out to the sheep who ran too far ahead of him, watching, always watching. Once over in the new pastureland, he stopped to let them eat, and rest. He sat down and leaned against a rock, and unstrapped his goatskin bag and put it on the ground beside him. Then he took out a flute, and made weird, beautiful sounds on it. His sling was tucked in his belt, and his rod[4] and his staff[5] were lying on the ground beside him. It was good to sit down. They'd come a long way, across jagged cliffs and crags and wastes rolling off into the desert. When the sheep were done eating he'd find them water, then lead them safely back to the fold. There they would be safe and snug inside the stone walls—but no door. He would roll up his cloak for a pillow and curl up in the doorway to protect them from the wild beasts—

He was the door. He would count them as they went in to see that each one was safely home. He knew them all by name.

It was a hard life, but it was a good life and he loved it. He was never lonely, for he was close to God. At night he would lie under the stars, his head on his folded cloak, and stare up into the sky. God was everywhere. He saw Him in the stars and moon by night and in the sun by day.[6] He saw Him in the storms, too—in the thunder and lightning. And he called the thunder the voice of God.[7] Everywhere

4. A stick about 30 inches long with a knob on one end.
5. Sort of like a walking cane with a crook on the end.
6. Psalm 19:1–8.

119

he looked he saw God's beauty and power. And in everything he heard, he heard God's voice.

His name was David. He was the youngest son in his large family. And he had no idea of the great destiny that God had planned for him.

In fact, none of these three people[8] knew it yet—but a great drama was about to begin.

Where to and What For?

"Get up!" God said to Samuel. "How long will you hang around mourning for Saul? You've mourned long enough—it's time to get going!" A shiver of excitement went through Samuel. What was God up to? What was going to happen? "Now," said God, "take a vial of olive oil, and go to Bethlehem."

"Yes, Lord."

"And find a man named Jesse."

"Yes, Lord. And—?"

"For I have selected one of his sons to be the new king."

Samuel slumped a minute. And all the ginger went out of him. "How can I do that, Lord?" he said. "If King Saul hears about it, he'll kill me!"

"Just take a heifer[9] with you," the Lord said, "and tell the people you've come to sacrifice to the Lord. Then call Jesse to the sacrifice and I'll do the rest."

Why, of course! Samuel made trips like that all the time. No one would suspect a thing! It *was* going to be easy.

He began to pack his duffel bag. And before you could say, "Hand me my sandals and walking cane," he had shuffled off to Bethlehem.

How Can It Happen?

When he got there, the elders of the city came to meet

7. Psalm 29.
8. Saul, Samuel, and David.
9. A young calf.

him. "Greetings," they said. "Is everything all right?"[10] And he said, "Oh, yes—I've just come to sacrifice unto the Lord. Get yourselves ready, and come with me to the sacrifice."

Well, everybody in town scurried to his house to get ready for the sacrifice.[11] It was good to have Samuel back in town again. And Samuel was glad to be back. But he was interested in one particular family—the one God had told him about.

Jesse's family.

So he hustled off to Jesse's house to look over Jesse's sons and choose the one God told him to.

And Who Is It?

But which one?

And how would he know?

Samuel began to look them over, one by one.

Eliab. Now there was a fine strapping lad. He looked as if he would make a great king. He was tall, he was nice looking, and he was the oldest. Surely he'd be the one the Lord had chosen.

"Wait a minute," the Lord said to Samuel. "Don't judge by his face, or because he's tall. This is not the one. I don't make decisions the way you do. Men just judge people by how they look. I judge them by what's in their hearts."

Oh. So that was it.

Next, Abinadab. Fine man, fine man. "No," said the Lord, "this is not the right one either."

Then Shammah.

Shammah? No.

Then the rest of them, one by one. The answer was no.

Samuel turned to Jesse. "Are these all there are? Do you have any more sons?"

"Oh!" said Jesse. "Yes! But he's the youngest. He's out in the fields watching the sheep."

10. They thought they might have done something wrong.
11. They washed and put on clean clothes.

121

"Send for him," Samuel said. "Now. For we will not sit down to eat until he arrives." So Jesse sent out for his youngest son.

And the rest of them waited. And waited.

And then finally he came in the room. A fine looking boy! He had reddish hair and fair skin—and beautiful eyes. And the Lord said, "This is the one. Anoint him."

It was David! The shepherd boy!

Samuel took the olive oil he'd brought with him. He poured it on David's head, before all of the family. He anointed David—what? He anointed him—*what?* Were they hearing right? Samuel anointed David—

To be a king!

David, the shepherd boy, was going to be the new king of Israel!

But.

Samuel went back to Ramah. David stayed where he was. And Saul had no idea what was going on. So how could all this happen?

It Could Happen—If God Wanted It To

Well, God wanted it to happen, and so of course it did. Right out of the blue. David was invited to the palace of the king. And in the strangest way.

A message came to Jesse's house. From the king.

What?

Yes, from the king. "Send me David, your son, who is with the sheep," it said.

How come?

Because King Saul's moods were becoming more and more violent is how come. When he plunged into despair, he plunged deeper now. When he fell into a rage, he was more uncontrollable now. No one, it seemed, could do anything with him.

And then someone thought of it.

Music!

122

"If only we can find someone who can play sweet music on the harp," the king's aides said, "maybe it would soothe him."

And Saul agreed.

Now it's a strange thing that someone at the king's palace would know about David, a shepherd boy. But someone did. And so David was sent for. Would he come?

Would he come! What an honor!

Jesse not only sent David to the king, but loaded him down with gifts. And David was suddenly transported from life as a shepherd boy in the country to life in the palace of the king.

—And God DID Want It To

The room they led David to was almost dark. He could hardly make out the objects in it at first. The important, bustling man hurried ahead of him and bowed low before a huge carved chair at the farther end.

There was a man in it.

He sat so still, David hadn't even seen him at first. He was a huge man, tall, with a massive[12] head. Handsome. And frightening. David's heart beat faster.

"King Saul," the man said in a nervous whisper. "We have brought the lad who's going to play for you."

The king didn't turn his head—not a feature on his face even flickered. He just sat, staring straight ahead at nothing. Except for his eyes, which seemed to burn, his face was without expression.

The nervous man turned toward David. "Play," he whispered.

David got his lyre[13] into position; he heard the door close softly behind him. He felt hot and his throat was dry and for a moment he just wanted to run. But his fingers found

12. Real big!
13. That's a small harp. It rhymes with "wire." Get it?

the strings of his lyre—and he drew from it the first soft haunting notes. And the music filled the room, every corner of it.

It splashed softly over everything, like liquid color, spilled and spreading. And it painted pictures—

It was—flat stones, scaled across a smooth brook, and water tumbling over rocks.

It was speckled shade dancing in the breeze.

It was a still pool being surprised by a pebble and breaking into a million crinkles and laughing.

It was sheep feeding on a hillside, and miles of green pasture.

It was the peace of God.

The late afternoon sun had reached that side of the palace, and it came in now through the high window, and it caught the glory of David's hair, like a flame.

There was a sigh. Slowly the king turned his head. The music stopped—and yet it was still there, filling the room.

"What is your name, lad?"

"My name is David, sire."

"David. Your music. Who taught you to play like that?"

"I am a shepherd, sire. I spend much time alone. I have my music—and God."

The king was silent for a long moment. And then softly, very softly, David began to play again. It was as if the two of them were all alone in the world. There was another sigh. And then the king was asleep. He was at peace at last.

He didn't know it, but a few feet away from him while he slept, sat the lad who was going to be the next king of Israel.

What About You?

All right, now. Let's say you have really committed yourself to the Lord—just turned everything over to Him so that He could have His way and work out His plan for your life. Have you ever wondered *how* He was going to do it? "I don't see how He's going to work this out; it just isn't possible!"

Well, you see, it works like this:

With God, all things are possible.

And He works through people.

And circumstances.

Just the way He did with David in this chapter.

He also works *on His own schedule,* so don't get impatient.

And you should, of course, obey the rules. Otherwise you might throw a monkey wrench in the works.

"Commit thy way unto the Lord; trust also in him; and he shall bring it to pass" (Ps. 37:5, *KJV*).

Carry this verse around with you for a few days. You might even decide to make it your "life's verse."

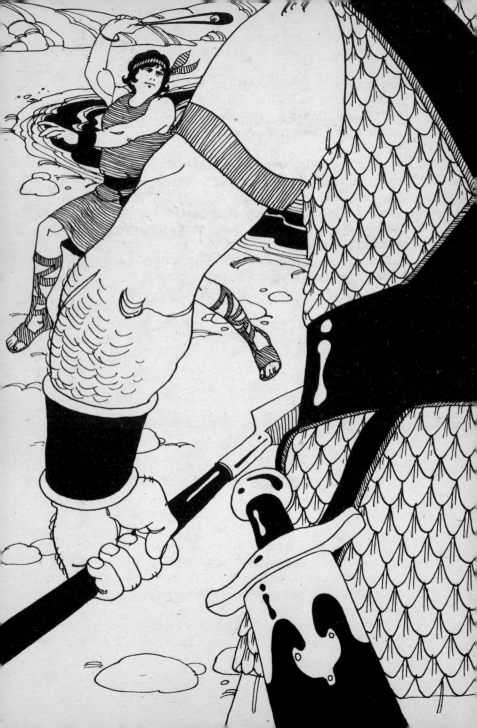

LICKING
THE BIG ONES
DOESN'T
JUST HAPPEN
1 Samuel 17:1-54

You Think the Contest Is Tough Now?

David sat bolt upright when he heard it. And all his senses
came alive. His hand reached for his sling, and his other
hand for his pouch, fishing for a stone. His sheep had heard
it too. They'd lifted their heads, startled awake from their
naps.

There it was again. A rustle, a twig snapping.

And then David saw the bear.

It stared at him, its eyes blood-red and angry.

He got up on one knee, slowly, carefully without making
a sound. He put a stone in his sling. Swung the sling over
his head. Timing had to be perfect. He took careful aim and—

Pftttttttt!

A stone flew through the air like a streak—

And hit its mark with perfect accuracy.

The bear had come looking for a sheep and instead had got a stone—right between the eyes. It staggered a few steps forward, and then its forelegs buckled. It was already lying on the ground by the time David reached its side. The sheep were all awake now, bleating—the older ones staggering to their feet. David quieted them with low throaty tones like a lullaby. He made sure the bear was dead. Then he hurried on down the path, calling his sheep after him. It would be foolish to stay. It was a she-bear and she might have a husband—a very angry husband.

Too bad to lose such a perfect spot. It was alongside a stream fed by spring rains high on the hills of Bethlehem. David moved quickly, his heart still pounding with excitement. He was wide, wide awake now.

Phew!

Not that it was anything new. It had happened before, many times. There were always bears about. And lions too. Once he had found a lion with one of his lambs in its mouth. And there was no time to be careful or quiet. In desperation he'd grabbed it by its whiskers and clubbed it to death with his rod.

He went on down the path, crooning to his still frightened sheep—every sense alert, watchful. There was always possible danger around the corner—every corner.

It was a lonely life, but you could never say it was a dull one.

When David wasn't watching sheep, he was in King Saul's fortress palace. He served in the palace on a part-time basis. He was sort of "on call." Whenever one of Saul's black and terrible moods descended upon him, David was sent for. He would leave his sheep with another shepherd, grab his lyre[1] and be off. And there, his music would fill the air—soft and haunting and tender, until Saul was lulled into quiet again.

1. Harp. Remember?

It's Going to Get Tougher

Saul was not the only one with black moods. The mood of the whole country was dark, as if a huge cloud had settled over it.

War.

The Philistines had invaded the land.

What? Did they have to go through that *again?*

Well, yes—and no.

It seemed like the same old dreary business, but this time it was different.

The Philistines were camped between Socoh in Judah and Azekah in Ephes-dammim. And Saul mustered his forces at Elah valley. So they were facing each other on opposite hills, with the valley between them. But this was not going to be a battle. This was going to be a contest. Ancient battles were sometimes settled by a contest between two warriors. And it looked as if that's the way this one was going to be settled. For the Philistines had already sent out their challenger.

And what a challenger!

When they saw him, the entire Israelite army cringed and shuddered like one man. Why he was over nine feet tall! He had on a coat of mail that looked as if it must have weighed at least two hundred pounds! And bronze leggings. And a bronze helmet as big as a peck basket! And a javelin! It was as big as a weaver's beam! And it was tipped with an iron spearhead that must have weighed twenty-five pounds if it weighed an ounce!

His armor-bearer walked before him. He looked like a dwarf, what with the size of the huge shield he was carrying, and the size of the giant behind him.

The giant raised his arms in the air. Everyone got quiet very suddenly.

"Do you need a whole army to settle this?" he bellowed. The silence was even greater. "Choose you a champion! Send him out here! We'll settle this in a single combat!"

No one dared answer him. No one moved.

129

"If your champion is able to kill me—you win!" he shouted. "But if I kill him—*we* win. And you will be our slaves!"

Not a man dared answer him. He waited a moment, then turned on his heel and stalked back again, his armor-bearer retreating behind him, walking backwards. Everyone sighed with relief.

This went on day after day.

The Big One Is Still Ahead

Time dragged on. The Israelite army stayed camped at Elah, shamed and silent, their families keeping them supplied with food.

And that's how David got into the act. For his brothers were there. And David's father, Jesse, was worried about them.

"David," he said, "take these field-rations to your brothers. Here's roasted grain, some loaves of bread—and here. Here's some cheese for their commander. See how the boys are getting along. And take their pledge.[2]

David packed the supplies and took off on the fifteen-mile trek from Bethlehem to the camp at Elah. As he arrived at the outskirts of the camp, the Israelite army was leaving for the battlefield. The excitement was high. David left his packages with the baggage officer and hurried through the ranks to find his brothers. He elbowed his way through the quivers and arrows and bows and slings and shields and spears, and men shouting battle cries and shouting at each other. And then, at last—his three brothers. All three were safe.

It's Getting Closer

And then it began. They were jostled backward as the men began to crowd back on them. What was going on? Then David saw.

The giant.

2. This was sort of like getting a receipt to see that the goods have been delivered.

He stepped out from the Philistine troops, started walking toward the valley between the two armies.

Who was *he?!?*, David wanted to know.

Everyone was talking at once.

"Have you seen the giant?"

"He has insulted the entire army of Israel."

"There's a reward from the king for whoever will kill him!"

"A reward—and one of the king's daughters for a wife!"

"And his whole family will be excused from paying taxes!"

Are You Ready to Take It On?

And then David heard his own voice. "Who is this heathen Philistine anyway?" he shouted, "that he's allowed to defy the armies of the living God?" What? Did that come out of him?

That came out of him.

His soldier brother Eliab was furious.

"What're you doing around here anyway?" he demanded.

"I came to—" David began.

"What about the sheep you're supposed to be taking care of?"

"What have I done now?"

"You're a cocky brat!"

"I was only asking a question!"

"You just came to see the battle!"

But David had a one-track mind. He turned to the other soldiers. "Who does this Philistine think he is that he should insult the living God?" he asked again.

Well, this *did* seem a bit cocky at that. And who was this kid who was talking like a king?

Yes, indeed.

Who *was* this kid who was talking like a king?

Here's Your Chance

The word began to spread. And sure enough, somebody told somebody who told somebody who told *somebody—*

—who told Saul.

And the next thing David knew, a messenger told him that King Saul wanted to see him.

By the time David faced Saul, his mind was made up. "Don't worry about this Philistine," he said, "I'll go out and fight him."

"You?" Saul said.

"I am a shepherd."

"How can a kid like you fight with a man like him?"

"Shepherds learn to be tough."

"You're only a boy. He's been in the army *since* he was a boy. Now he's a giant."

"I have killed lions and bears with a single shot. I've gone after them with my club and taken my lambs right out of their mouths. I've caught them by the jaw and clubbed them to death. I've done this to both lions and bears."

Saul sighed patiently. "But he is a giant. In armor of bronze and iron."

"I'll do the same thing to him too," said David, "for he has defied the armies of the living God."

Saul was silent, remembering. The living God.

And Samuel.

And his own youth.

"The Lord who saved me from the claws of the lion and the bear will save me from this Philistine," David was saying. Saul sighed.

"All right," he said. "Go."

Did You Mean All Your Big-Talk?

He signaled for an aide to bring his armor. "And the Lord be with you," he added, and there was a great sadness in his voice.

The armor of course turned out to be ridiculous. It was too heavy, it was too unwieldy.[3] David felt as if he'd been

3. Hard to handle.

put in a cage. "I can hardly move," he said, as he began to take the things off. Saul nodded. Very well, then, let David go as he was, without armor.

This Is It!

David strode out toward the valley.

"I defy the armies of Israel!" the giant was shouting.

David was crouching by a small brook, carefully fishing out five smooth stones. He put them in his pouch.

"Send me a man who will fight with me!" the giant bellowed.

David straightened up, putting the last of the five stones in his pouch as he walked toward the giant. The talking and shouting of both armies simmered down to zero as David got into plain sight of all.

And Goliath stopped in his tracks.

And who was *this?* This "great warrior" coming at him with a staff and a leather sling? This apple-cheeked boy! This *kid!* Had everybody gone mad? He looked at David as if David was an ant he intended to squash. "Am I a dog?" he roared, "that you come at me with a stick?"

David kept coming toward him.

"By Dagon, I'll have your hide!"

David kept coming.

"Come over here and I'll feed you to the birds!"

They both stopped short for a moment, eyeing each other.

Head-on!

"You come to me with a sword and a spear," David shouted back. "But I come to you in the name of the Lord!"

Goliath opened his mouth to shout—and closed it again. David hadn't finished.

"This day the Lord will conquer you!"

Goliath's eyes boggled.

"And I'll cut off your head and feed *you* to the birds! And your men!"

Goliath's roar turned into a gurgle. He was purple with rage. And speechless. David reached into his pouch for a stone. "The battle is the Lord's!" he shouted. "He will give you into our hands!" And he ran toward Goliath with the grace of a panther, loading his sling as he went. Then he stopped.

And took aim.

"And all the world will know that there's a God in Israel!" he shouted.

You Did It, You Did It!

He swung his sling in a circle and—

Pfffffffffft!

The stone streaked through the air.

Goliath looked astonished, almost comical as he stood for a second, and then staggered forward.

His armor-bearer sprang out of the way.

And Goliath fell to the ground, a stone embedded in his forehead.

Then everything was in an uproar! The shout that went up from the Philistines was one of shock and terror as they knocked each other over to get out of there.

The Israelites stood numb with shock for a second. And then the roar that went up filled the valley and bounced against the mountains on both sides. It was a roar of unbelief!

David ran toward the fallen giant. He took his own sword out of its sheath. And—

WHAM!

Cut off his head.

At the same time, the Israelite army was suddenly galvanized[4] into action. Their roar turned into a shout of triumph as they scrambled down the hill, across the valley and after the Philistines.

David was surrounded with all kinds of help now. The

4. Started moving—really moving.

soldiers asking him if he was all right, brushing him off, helping him to strip the armor from the dead giant. And then taking him to Saul.

David walked toward the tent of the king. He was not the apple-cheeked boy now. He was not the lad who served the king part-time and then went back home to tend his father's sheep. And he was not the kid brother. He was the hero of the day.

Nothing would ever be the same again. Ever.

David was at Jerusalem now—full time.

What About You?

The problems you're facing right now are the lions and the bears. They're for you to practice on so you will grow strong—so when the giants come along you'll be prepared. Like David, you'll be prepared physically by good living and hard work and keeping the training rules. And you'll have your talents polished to a standstill because you've been practicing. And you'll be prepared spiritually too, by spending time alone with God and by studying His Word.

"Prepare your hearts unto the Lord, and serve him only: and he will deliver you out of the hand of the Philistines" (1 Sam. 7:3, *KJV*).

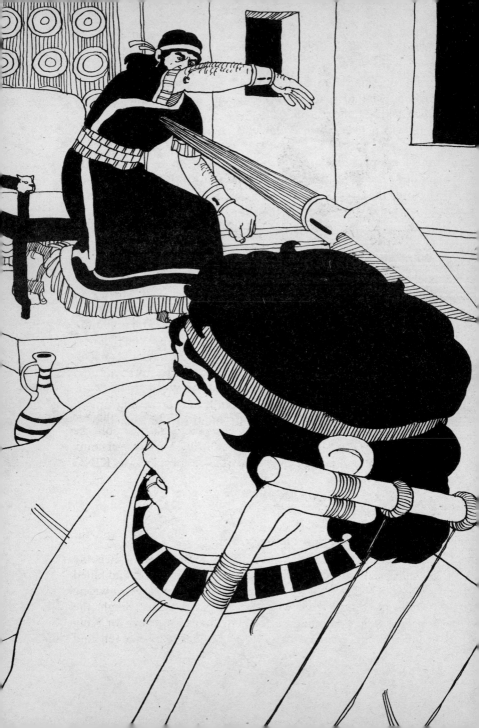

THE LITTLE MITE THAT GREW

1 Samuel 18—20

In the beginning, everything was going first rate. Saul was the king. No matter what had happened, he was still the ruler. And nobody questioned his authority. He had won many battles. He had power. Everyone obeyed him. He was KING and no mistake.

Nothing could go wrong now.

Or could it?

The Little Mite That Grew

It started with such a little thing. It happened when the victorious Israelite army returned home after David had killed Goliath. Naturally it was a cause to celebrate. Nothing wrong with that. In all the towns the soldiers passed through, the people came streaming out of their houses to cheer for King Saul for the great victory. Most of them were women and children.[1] They were singing and cheering and dancing for joy, with tambourines and cymbals. And it was a pretty crashing, tinkling, smashing business. The din was terrific.

What was wrong with this? Well, it was what they were singing and shouting *about* that was wrong. "Saul has slain his thousands," they sang.

And then—the bombshell.

"And David, HIS TEN THOUSANDS!"

Oh-oh.

"What's this?" Saul thought to himself. "They credit me with thousands. And they credit David with *ten* thousands? What's all the shouting about *him* for? He's not *that* much. Hmmmmf. Next they'll be making him their king."

It didn't seem like much. Just a little angry thought. It was like a little mite, smaller than a fruit fly. What harm could it do?

David, of course, was very happy. He was happy over the cheering. And he was happy over the victory God had given him. It had never crossed his mind that anybody would *not* be happy. Why, there was everything to cheer about.

And besides, he had met Jonathan.

Jonathan. The king's son.

Some friendships grow slowly. And some friendships just seem to bust out all over, right on the spot. That's what this friendship did. David and Jonathan loved each other on sight. The minute they saw each other, they thought: "Brothers." And that's what they swore to be. Blood brothers. And Jonathan sealed the pact by giving David his robe and his sword and his bow and his belt.[2] Now David had a friend who loved him more than any of his own brothers did. And a good thing, too. That David had a friend, that is. As it turned out, he needed one.

1. Most of the men had been in the battle.
2. This was a great honor, to show Jonathan's high regard for David.

For the little mite was there, ever so tiny. And the name of that mite was JEALOUSY.

The Care and Feeding of Mites

Now if you want jealousy to grow, you can't neglect it. You have to *think* about it. And *mope* about it. Every spare minute.

And this is exactly what King Saul did. He thought about it. And moped about it. And he watched David like a cat watches a mouse. What was David up to now? Was he getting too much attention? Were people being too nice to him? Was he getting all the favors? Jealous. Jealous.

Watch. Watch. Watch.

Mope.

Sure enough. Saul moped himself right into another black mood. This was a bad one. He began to rave like a madman. There was nothing to do, his advisers thought, but send for David.

He watched through narrowed eyes as David ran his fingers over the strings on his lyre,[3] and the sweet haunting sounds of the first song filled the air. David, he thought. Apple-cheeked, healthy, handsome—and *happy*. Saul sat there, toying with his javelin. The Lord had left him, he knew that.[4] That's why everything was going wrong. But that wasn't the worst part. The worst part was that now the Lord was with *David*. Saul's hand tightened on his javelin. How dare David be apple-cheeked, healthy, handsome—and *happy!* And with one mighty H-E-A-V-E!—he hurled the javelin at David as if he would pin him to the wall!

Then everything happened at once. David jumped aside just in time. The music stopped. And the assistants came running, and bustled David quickly out of the room, to safety.

"Don't let him come back!" Saul shouted after them. "I

3. You guessed it, a harp.
4. But he still wasn't sorry that he had disobeyed!

139

don't want to see his face again! And—and—demote him to the rank of captain!"

Well, of course, Saul's orders were obeyed. After all, he was the king. But this little scrap became a public scandal when the gossips got hold of it. Now David's name was on the tip of everyone's tongue. He was better known than ever.

But the little mite was growing.

The Little Mite Begins to Scheme

Now it's bad enough to be jealous when you just mope and fume and let it go at that. But when you are jealous and you deliberately plot mischief, then you're really in trouble. And this is exactly what King Saul began to look for an opportunity to do.

His chance came when he realized that his daughter Michal and David had fallen in love.

Ah HAH. This was it.

"I'm delighted!" he said. "Now you can be my son-in-law!" And that was the rub. For Saul knew quite well that David did not have enough wealth to pay the dowry[5] for the daughter of a king. And David said just what Saul had hoped he would say. "But, sir, how can a man like me from an unknown family find enough dowry to marry the daughter of a king? No way!"—and walked right into the trap. This is what Saul had been waiting for.

Dowry? Dowry? Why, he didn't want a dowry! The only dowry he wanted was one hundred Philistines. Vengeance on his enemies was all he wanted. Or that was what he wanted David to *think*. What he *really* had in mind was that David would be killed in the fight.

That was what Saul *wanted*, but that's not the way it turned out. For there was one little hitch in his plans. David gathered

5. A bridal gift. And presents for her parents and brothers too. And for a king's daughter they'd better be expensive!

some men and went out and killed *two* hundred Philistines. And came back looking healthier than ever.

Aauuuuuugh.

So instead of getting rid of David, Saul's shenanigans[6] were making him even more popular. Saul was frantic.

The More You Feed It, the Bigger It Gets

The situation was getting desperate. Saul pulled no punches now. He came right out with it. He urged his aides and his son Jonathan to assassinate David. Including Jonathan in the deal was a big mistake. For Jonathan was not about to let his friend get killed.

He cornered David at the first opportunity.

"Listen closely. Don't interrupt me. And don't ask any questions. I have to talk fast," he whispered. David nodded. "Tomorrow morning," Jonathan went on, "find a hiding place out in the fields. I'll ask my father to take a walk out there with me. I'll talk to him about you. Then I'll tell you everything he says."

The two friends parted quickly. There was no time to say any more.

Well, Saul did agree to go for a walk with Jonathan. And he was in one of his better moods. And Jonathan lost no time in getting to the point.

"David has never harmed you," he pleaded. "He's helped you."

Saul walked in silence, staring at the ground.

"Have you forgotten about the time he risked his life to kill Goliath?" Jonathan went on. "And the Lord gave us a great victory because of it?"

Saul still didn't answer.

"You were happy about it then," Jonathan said. "Why should you want him murdered now? There's no reason for it."

6. Dirty tricks.

141

Saul stopped in his tracks and looked at Jonathan.

"All right," he said finally. "I'll make you a promise. David shall not be killed. Now let's go back in."

"You go ahead, father," Jonathan said. "I—eh—I have some things to do."

Saul was no sooner out of sight than—

"Psssst. David. Are you in there? You can come out now."

David scrambled out from the brush. And Jonathan told him everything that had happened. "You can come back with me now," he said. "There's nothing to fear. Everything will be as it was before."

And David did go back. And everything was as it had been before.

Or was it?

—And Sneaky, Too

It was quiet in the king's quarters. Saul was sitting, relaxed, listening. And David was playing the lyre.[7] There had been another brief war and David had been successful again. But now he was back. And Saul was as warm and friendly as a basket of chips. When suddenly—

Saul lifted the javelin and—

Wooooooooosh!

David ducked and the javelin went into the wall with a great thud. And stayed there, quivering. It was still quivering a few minutes later when Saul's aides came rushing in. But David wasn't there. He'd gone rushing into the night. By now he was halfway to his own house . . .

It's Growing and Growing

It was later that night. David was in his home, staring out the window. His wife Michal was wringing her hands. "You must get away, tonight," she said. "If you don't, you'll be dead by morning."

7. Yep.

142

There was no use arguing with her; David knew she was right.

"They'll kill you when you go out in the morning."

Yes.

A few minutes later a shadowy figure sneaked through the garden, stooping, keeping to the shadows. Then, once a safe distance away, straightened, ran into the night. It was David. Michal had helped him out a window.

The next morning there was a pounding on the door, and the soldiers asking for David.

"He's sick," Michal said. "He can't go with you. He can't get out of bed."

"Can't get out of bed!" Saul bellowed when they told him. "Then bring him here! Bed and all!"

So the soldiers came back to get him. And sure enough, there he was, under the blankets, his head on his pillow, sleeping soundly.

They had him for sure this time.

This was it.

They pulled the covers back and—

It was a wooden house god! And the head was a thatch of goat's hair!

Auuuuuugh!

Saul was purple with rage! But if he could have stamped his foot right through the floor like Rumpelstiltskin, it would have done no good. For David was already on his way to Ramah to see the prophet Samuel.

The Zig-Zag Game

This looked like a fight to the finish. The action got faster. There was no more sparring or going into clinches. Now they were bobbing and weaving and zigging and zagging, like fighters trying to keep from getting punched.

Zig! Samuel took David to Naioth.[8]

8. Probably the school where Samuel taught prophets.

Zag! Saul sent soldiers to capture him.

Zig! They failed.

Zag! Saul sent more soldiers.

Zig! They failed.

Zag! He tried it again.

Zig! You guessed it.

Zag! Now Saul himself went to find David.

Zig! David escaped again. And found his friend Jonathan!

And what kind of a mood was Saul in now?

David and Jonathan got into a huddle to plan their strategy.

Of all the kings of Israel, Saul must have set some kind of a record for moodiness. He changed so often that it was impossible to keep up with him. One thing certain about his moods: If you didn't like the one he was in, you could hang around for a while—it would change.

This is what David and Jonathan talked about. What was Saul's mood *now?*

"I don't think he's planning to kill you," Jonathan said. "He always tells me everything. Even little things. I know he'd tell me."

"He would *not,*" said David. "He knows about our friendship."

"I can't believe he'd try to kill you."

"Jonathan! Face the truth! I'm only one step away from death. And you know it."

"All right," Jonathan sighed. "Tell me what I can do."

David thought a minute. "Tomorrow is the first day of the yearly sacrifice feast. I won't go. I'll hide outside."

"Yes?"

"And if your father asks for me—tell him I've gone home to Bethlehem for a family reunion. If he says, 'Fine!'—I'll know that everything's all right. But if he's angry, I'll know he's still planning to kill me."

"I'll do it all. Just as you say," said Jonathan.

But there was only one problem. How would Jonathan let David know what happened?

They decided to use their old hideout. "Be at the hideout where you were before," said Jonathan. "Over by the stone pile. I'll come out for some target practice. And bring a boy with me."

"Yes?" David listened tensely.

"And I'll shoot three arrows, as though I were shooting at a target. Now listen carefully. If I shoot them in *front* of the stone pile, I'll send the boy to bring them back. And I'll tell him, 'They're on *this side.*' That will mean all is well—there's no trouble. BUT."

"Yes," said David. "I'm way ahead of you."

"If I shoot them *past* the stone pile, I'll yell at the lad. 'Go farther! The arrows are still up ahead of you!' And that means—"

"That means I get out of there as fast as I can," said David.

"Yes. You run for your life, David."

They looked at each other a long moment, these two young men who loved each other. And they clasped hands and they swore to be friends forever, no matter what happened.

Then they turned away from each other sadly. There was nothing to do now—but wait for tomorrow.

The Monster Is Full-Grown

The day of the sacrificial feast should have been one of great joy in the house of the king. But instead, people were edgy and cautious, as if they were waiting for a storm to break. Saul was nippy as he sat down at the table. And the gloom hung in the air like a black cloud.

Jonathan waited. Perhaps his father wouldn't ask about David. After all, he'd just finished chasing him all over the country. Why would he expect David to be here?

But with Saul, you never knew *what* he would expect.

Jonathan watched his father cautiously.

The day passed.

Nothing happened.

Phew!

It was on the second day of the feast that everything exploded.

Jonathan was still watching his father cautiously, waiting. Even so, it brought him up with a jolt.

"Why hasn't David been here?" Saul said. "He wasn't here yesterday and he isn't here today."

"Here goes," thought Jonathan. He cleared his throat and plunged in. "He asked me if he could go to Bethlehem. It's a family celebration," he said. "I told him to go ahead."

Saul glared at Jonathan like a madman. Everyone sat, scalps aprickling.

Then it came.

"You—you—pfooooooooooo!!!" shrieked Saul. His face was purple and his eyes were bulging out of his head. "Don't you think I know that you want this—this—this NOBODY to be king in your place? And putting you to shame? As long as that fellow is alive, you'll never be king! Now go get him so I can kill him! GO GET HIMMMMM!"

Jonathan was angry too. "What has he done?" he cried, "Why should he be killed?!?"

And Saul picked up his javelin and hurled it straight at Jonathan—straight at his own son!

Jonathan ducked.

Then he arose from the table.

Then he walked out of the room, trembling with anger and shame.

He didn't eat the rest of that day. His hurt and shame overwhelmed him. And that night, he lay staring into the darkness, unable to sleep. He was sick with grief. He knew that the next morning he would have to send David away.

The End of the Chase

It was a bleak[9] morning. Jonathan got up early, took a

9. Like from gloomsville.

146

servant boy with him, and went off to archery practice, dragging his feet on the way. For he knew what was ahead.

He went to the field to the spot he and David had decided on. "Start running!" he told the boy, as he strung his bow, "so you can find the arrows as I shoot them." And he shot a couple of arrows for the boy to chase. The boy ran after them, and Jonathan strung his bow again. His arm trembled and his eyes stung with tears. This was the signal arrow.

He took a deep breath and pulled his bowstring way back—and shot the arrow, true and swift, right over the boy's head. Then as the boy got up to the first arrow that had been shot, Jonathan gave David the signal. "Go on! Go on!" he yelled to the boy. "I shot one just ahead of you! It's *way up ahead of you!*" That was the signal they'd agreed on, but Jonathan wanted to make sure that David got it. "Hurry!" he shouted. "Hurry! Don't wait!"

He watched the boy run beyond the pile of rocks. He saw him stoop over, pick up the arrow. And he watched him as he came running back. Then he dropped his arms to his sides. All the strength had gone out of him.

The boy ran up to Jonathan, panting, out of breath. He didn't have the slightest idea of the part he had played in this drama. Only Jonathan and David knew.

Jonathan gave the boy his bow and the rest of the arrows. "You may go back," he said. "We're through for the day."

Jonathan watched the pile of rocks as the boy took the arrows and went on his way. David came out from behind them.

He had heard. He knew.

Jonathan could keep the tears back no longer. They walked toward each other. They put their hands on each other's shoulders. And they both wept together. "Remember," Jonathan said, "we have entrusted ourselves to God forever. Some day, when we have children, we will trust them to God too."

David nodded. They looked at each other for a moment. Then David turned away.

Jonathan went slowly back to his father's house, shamed and grieved. Shamed for his father—grieved for the loss of his friend. The only bright spot was that he knew that he was in God's hands. And so was his friend. And God knew what He was doing. He would take care of them both.

You Grew a Monster? Now You're Stuck with It

Saul was left alone with his monster. He had been feeding it since it was a tiny mite—just a thought, just a twinge.

Jealousy.

And it had grown and grown, until it had filled his whole life. Once his goal had been to be a king—a good king. Now his only goal in life was to kill David.

He had nothing left in life now—only his monster. There was no room for anything else.

David went on his way, not knowing where he was going. But of one thing he was sure.

He was in God's hands.

He made his way across the fields—a fugitive—hunted, not daring to go home.

But one day he would be a king!

What About You?

Is jealousy eating you? It can, you know. It nibbles at your personality and your sweet disposition and it grows and grows until it becomes a monster.[10]

Recognize jealousy for what it is. It is your cruelest enemy. And recognize it for what it does. It spoils you as a Christian and as a person.

"A relaxed attitude lengthens a man's life; jealousy rots it away." Who said that? Why it's in the Word of God (Prov. 14:30, *TLB*). So if jealousy is nibbling at you, run, don't walk, to God and ask Him to take care of it. He is the only one who can help you.

---

10. And people call *you* a little monster too—a thorough stinker.

HOLD ON
A MINUTE—
THERE'S ONE
MORE THING

What did you think of the people in this book? Each one handled the rules in his own way. They ran the gamut[1] from A to Z.

Which one of them do you think you are like? Were you born to be a leader but forgot that you're supposed to *work* at it? Do you have to stay on the sidelines and you've forgotten that God is there too? Did you get off to a smashing start and now you've run out of gas? Do you break the rules? Bend them a little? Throw them out altogether and make your own?

Or do you keep them?

There was a sailor (and this is a true story) who had never been on speaking terms with God. And then someone told him about God's great gift of His Son. And he accepted that gift, and Jesus became his Saviour, and he became a Christian.

1. The whole works!

Now, of course, he didn't have the faintest idea about how to act as a Christian, and he certainly didn't know the first thing about how to pray. But he figured it out the best way he knew how. And this is what he did.

"Every morning when I get up," he said, "I say, 'Good morning, Lord.' And then I salute. And I say—'Reporting for duty, Sir.' "

How *about* that? Isn't that stupendous?[2]

He had put the whole thing in a nutshell. There was work to be done, and rules to keep. Being a Christian didn't mean just sliding by. "Reporting for *duty*, Sir," he'd said.

He had already obeyed the first commandment that made him a Christian. "And this is his commandment, That we should believe on the name of his Son Jesus Christ . . ." (1 John 3:23, *KJV*).

And now that he was a Christian, he knew that all the rules were put there by God.[3]

In his own way, he had put it all together.

Reporting for duty, Sir.

This is what it's all about!

2. Very very great!
3. Read Romans 13:1–5.

150